PB96-916201
NTSB/HAR-96/01

NATIONAL TRANSPORTATION SAFETY BOARD

WASHINGTON, D.C. 20594

HIGHWAY ACCIDENT REPORT

HIGHWAY/RAIL GRADE CROSSING COLLISION
NEAR SYCAMORE, SOUTH CAROLINA
MAY 2, 1995

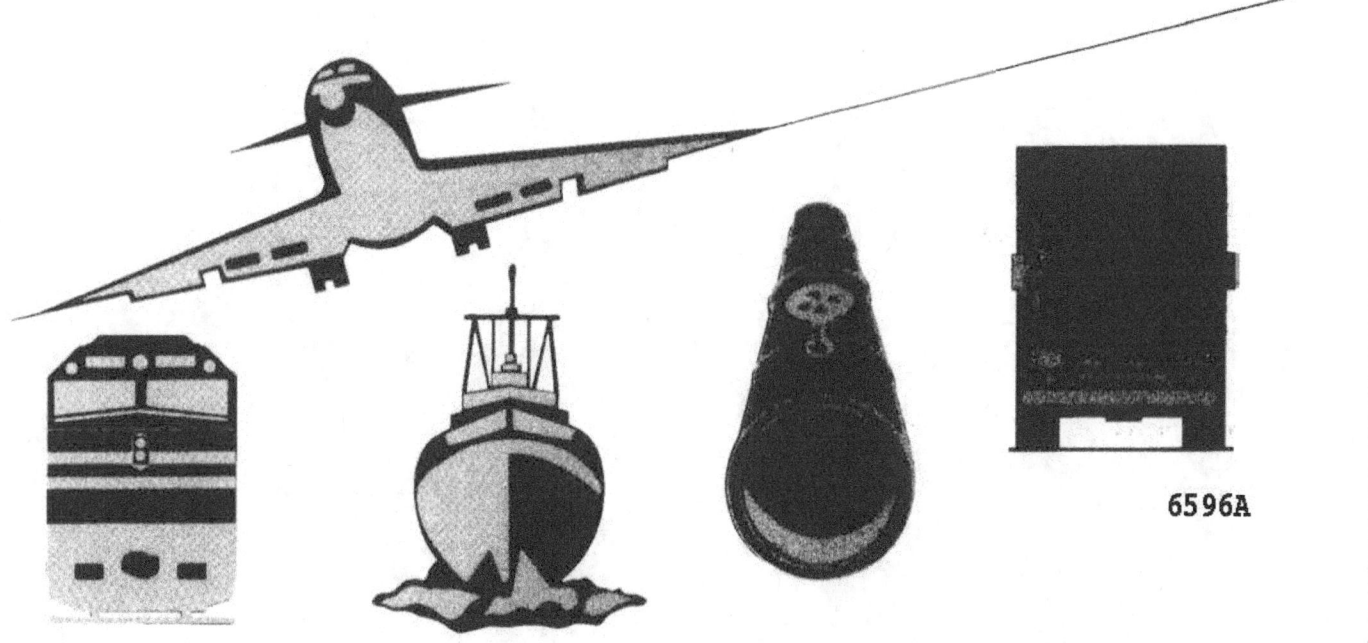

6596A

Abstract: On May 2, 1995, a truck consisting of a tractor and a lowbed semitrailer became lodged on a high-profile (hump) railroad grade crossing near Sycamore, South Carolina. About 35 minutes later, the truck was struck by southbound Amtrak train No. 81 en route from New York City to Tampa, Florida. No deaths resulted from the accident, but 33 persons sustained minor injuries. Combined property damage to the truck and train exceeded $1 million.

The following issues in grade crossing safety are discussed in this report: identification and warnings of hump crossings, emergency notifications at grade crossings, and adequacy of training for commercial drivers.

As a result of its investigation, the National Transportation Safety Board issued recommendations to the Secretary of Transportation; the Federal Highway Administration; the American Public Transit Association; the American Association of Motor Vehicle Administrators; the American Trucking Associations, Inc.; the American Short Line Railroad Association; Operation Lifesaver, Inc.; all Class I railroads and railroad systems; and O&J Gordon Trucking Company.

The National Transportation Safety Board is an independent Federal agency dedicated to promoting aviation, railroad, highway, marine, pipeline, and hazardous materials safety. Established in 1967, the agency is mandated by Congress through the Independent Safety Board Act of 1974 to investigate transportation accidents, determine the probable causes of the accidents, issue safety recommendations, study transportation safety issues, and evaluate the safety effectiveness of government agencies involved in transportation. The Safety Board makes public its actions and decisions through accident reports, safety studies, special investigation reports, safety recommendations, and statistical reviews.

HIGHWAY/RAIL GRADE CROSSING COLLISION NEAR SYCAMORE, SOUTH CAROLINA MAY 2, 1995

HIGHWAY ACCIDENT REPORT

Adopted: March 11, 1996
Notation 6596A

**NATIONAL
TRANSPORTATION
SAFETY BOARD**

Washington, D.C. 20594

CONTENTS

EXECUTIVE SUMMARY

About 2:35 a.m. on May 2, 1995, National Railroad Passenger Corporation (Amtrak) train No. 81, the Silver Star, on its southbound run from New York, New York, to Tampa, Florida, struck an O&J Gordon Trucking Company tractor-lowbed semitrailer combination that had been lodged for 30 to 35 minutes on a rural, high-vertical-profile (hump)[1], passive[2] grade crossing about 1 mile north of Sycamore, South Carolina. At the time of the accident, the train was using a single main line track belonging to CSX Transportation, Inc. (CSXT). The two locomotive units and 14 cars of the 16-car consist derailed. The tractor and semitrailer were substantially damaged. No fire ensued.

The train was carrying 279 passengers, 9 service crewmembers, and 5 operating crew members. Thirty-three persons sustained minor injuries. Combined property damage to the train and truck exceeded $1 million.

The Safety Board determines that the probable cause of this accident was the motor carrier's failure to provide to the driver appropriate guidance to respond to emergency situations. This led to the truckdriver's failure both to understand that the substandard profile of the Boogaloo Road grade crossing was incompatible with the truck he was operating, and to notify the appropriate railroad and emergency personnel of the blocked crossing. Contributing to the accident was the absence of emergency notification information that the driver may have used to notify the railroad of the blocked crossing.

In its investigation of this accident, the Safety Board addressed the following issues in grade crossing safety: identification and warnings of hump crossings, emergency notifications at grade crossings, and adequacy of training for commercial drivers.

As a result of this investigation, the Safety Board issued recommendations to the Secretary of Transportation; the Federal Highway Administration; the American Public Transit Association; the American Association of Motor Vehicle Administrators; the American Trucking Associations, Inc.; the American Short Line Railroad Association; Operation Lifesaver, Inc.; all Class I railroads and railroad systems; and O&J Gordon Trucking Company.

---

[1]A grade crossing where the railroad tracks are significantly elevated above the approaching roadway, creating a "hump" profile.

[2]A grade crossing with passive devices such as signs but lacking other visual or audible signaling devices or gates that automatically activate when a train approaches.

INVESTIGATION

The Accident

Pre-Accident -- About 7:00 a.m. on May 1, 1995, a truckdriver reported for work at O&J Gordon Trucking Company (O&J) in Estill, South Carolina. During the day, he made several local trips hauling logs. About 5:00 p.m., the truckdriver's employer called him on the two-way radio and dispatched him to Walterboro, South Carolina, where he was to pick up a lowbed semitrailer and haul some logging equipment.

The truckdriver stated that, upon arriving in Walterboro, he hooked up his tractor to the semitrailer and cranked the trailer's landing gear fully upward until it locked. As he was directed to do, he then loaded a Timberjack (a piece of logging machinery) onto the semitrailer and took it to Steedman, South Carolina, arriving about 9:00 p.m. He said that after unloading the machinery at Steedman, he drove to Lexington, South Carolina, where he was to pick up another Timberjack and return it and the semitrailer to Walterboro.

The driver said he arrived in Lexington about 11:00 p.m. He said he attempted to load the Timberjack onto the semitrailer, but the Timberjack's engine would not start. About midnight, he decided to return to his residence near Sycamore, about 75 miles away, to get some sleep. He said he did not consider staying in Lexington because he had no money for a motel. He said he decided against unhooking the semitrailer and leaving it in Lexington because he thought the trailer would not be secure there.

From Lexington, the driver traveled southeast on I-26 to U.S. 321, then drove south toward Sycamore. (See figure 1.) He said he stopped in Neeses, South Carolina, for a short nap, and that it was about 2:00 a.m. when he turned right off of U.S. 321 onto the unpaved roadway leading to his residence. He said that, after making the turn, he drove in first gear about 100 feet to an unlighted, passive, hump grade crossing located about 300 feet east of his residence and about 1 mile north of Sycamore.

The truckdriver stated that when he reached the grade crossing, he stopped and looked both ways before crossing. He said he continued forward over the tracks, looking in his side mirror at the semitrailer side marker lights, until he heard something scraping and felt the truck stop suddenly. He tried to back up, but the truck would not move. He said he got out of the tractor and saw that the semitrailer had about 2 to 3 inches of ground clearance. He did not notice that the semitrailer's landing gear, which protruded below the frame rails of the semitrailer, had become embedded in the crossing's asphalt surface. (See figure 2.)

1

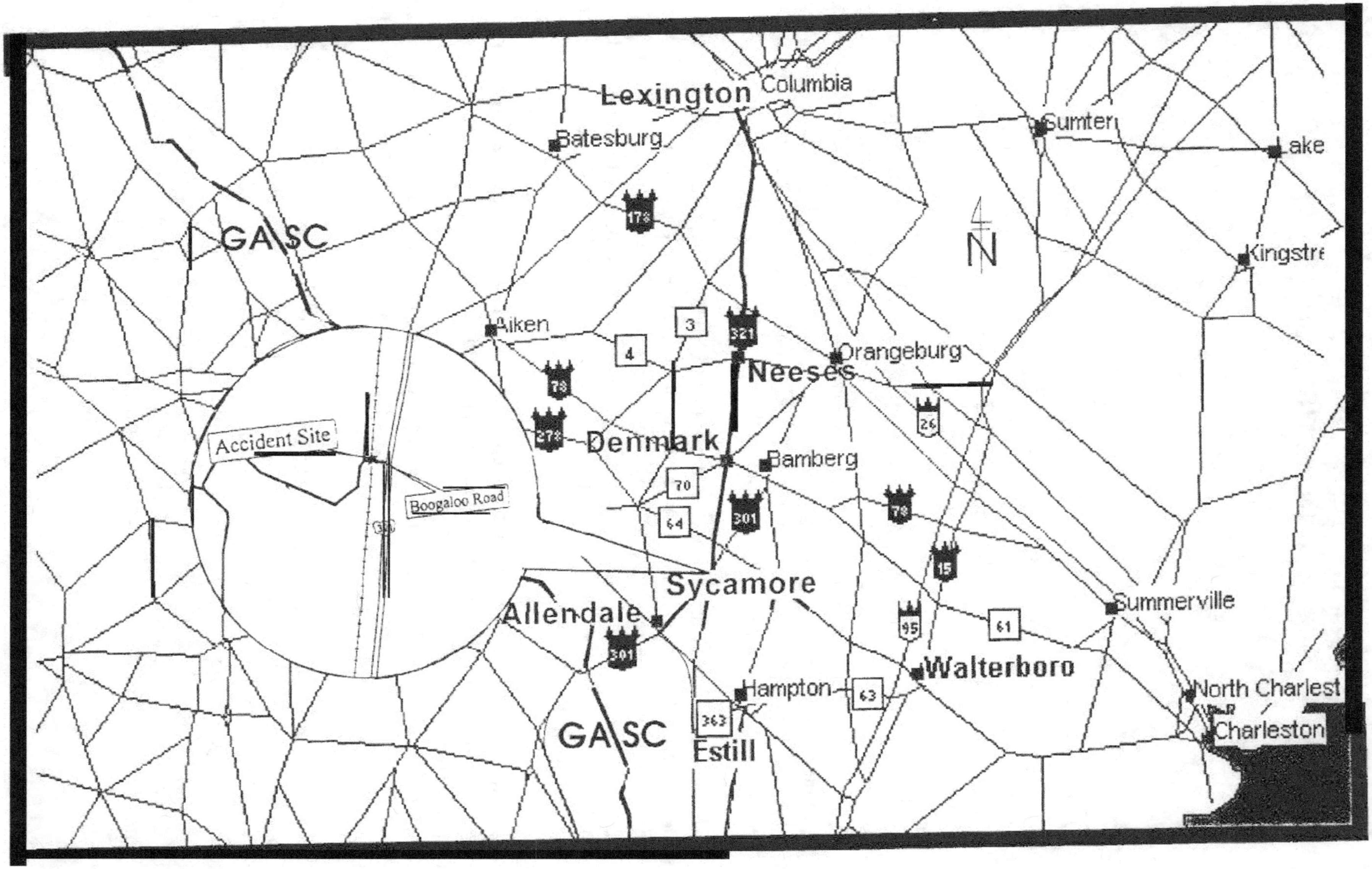

Figure 1-- Location of the accident

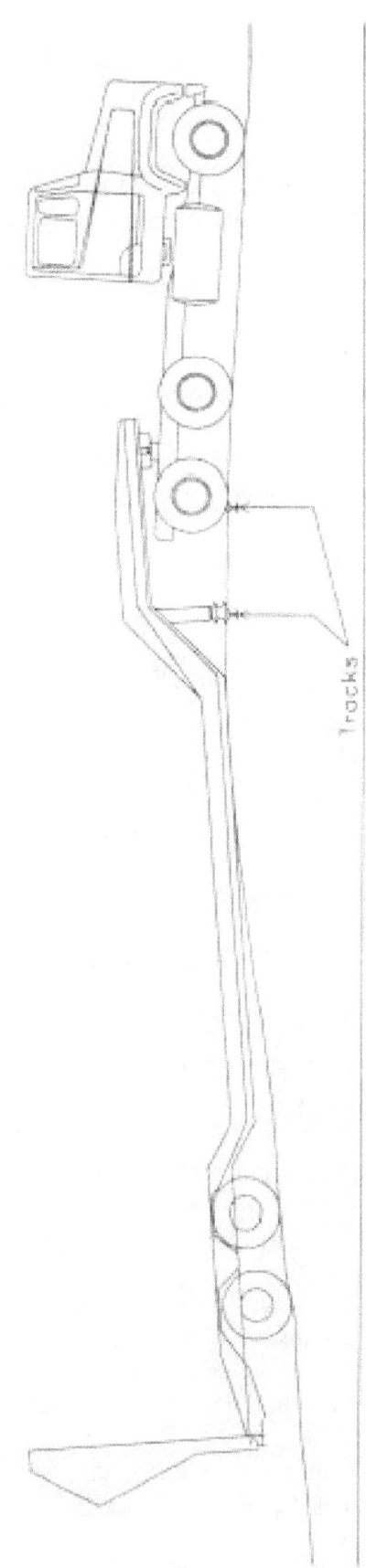

Figure 2 -- Vertical profile of accident crossing

He got back into the tractor and again tried, without success, to move the truck either forward or backward off the crossing. He said he engaged the rear axle differential to supply power to all four rear wheels, but the wheels simply spun without moving the truck. Unable to move the truck, the truckdriver said he tried unsuccessfully to uncouple the semitrailer.

The truckdriver stated that, while he was unaware of the train schedules at the crossing, he was concerned about getting the truck off the tracks. In fact, at about 2:14 a.m., while the truckdriver was attempting to move his lodged vehicle, Amtrak train 81, with 16 cars and 279 passengers, departed Denmark, South Carolina, on CSXT single main line track southbound toward the blocked crossing. The truckdriver said he tried to use his two-way radio to contact the carrier's office; however, the office was closed and no one responded. Also, he stated that during the previous day he had tried several times to use the cellular telephone in the tractor, but that each time the phone indicated that it was out of its service range.

The truckdriver went to his brother's house about 200 feet from the crossing, awakened him, and requested his assistance. The truckdriver's brother drove his pickup truck from his house to the crossing, where the two men attempted, without success, to use the truck to pull the semitrailer rearward off the track.

About 2:30 a.m., a cousin to the brothers, who lived about 100 feet from the crossing, was awakened by his dog barking. He said he saw the truck at the crossing, got dressed, and when he walked outside to see what was happening, he saw his truckdriver cousin trying to free the truck. He stated that within two minutes of coming out of the house he saw the headlight of a train coming from the north, and he yelled to the truckdriver that a train was coming. The truckdriver stated that he asked his cousin for a flashlight so he could look in his truck for reflective triangles, which he said he intended to place 10 to 20 feet apart on the tracks in an effort to stop the train. Unable to locate the triangles and hearing the train's horn, the truckdriver began waving his arms and running down the middle of the tracks toward the train. The truckdriver's brother said he heard his cousin's yell and ran across the highway to safety.

According to the train's assistant engineer, who was operating the train immediately prior to the accident, Amtrak train 81 was approaching Sycamore at about 79 mph with its headlights in the bright position and its ditch lights on. The assistant engineer said that as the train approached a whistle post (which was located 1,335 feet from the crossing), he sounded the horn. He said he then noticed someone waving his arms and saw a semitrailer on the tracks ahead. He placed the brakes in emergency application and continued to sound the horn until impact occurred. The force of the impact knocked him to the floor.

The engineer, who was sitting on the opposite side of the locomotive cab, said he also saw the semitrailer blocking the tracks. He said he pulled the emergency brake handle on the right side of the engine compartment about the same time the assistant engineer placed the train into emergency braking; he then went to the floor, bracing himself for the imminent impact.

The conductor and assistant conductors aboard the train said that they were in the dining car when they heard and felt the train brakes go into emergency. Eight on-board service (OBS) crewmembers were in the slumber coach, and one was in the sleeper car. The conductor said that when the impact occurred, he noted that the time was 2:35 a.m.

Collision -- Amtrak train 81 struck the right side of the semitrailer. The impact caused both locomotives and 14 of the 16-car consist to derail. The lead locomotive came to rest on the west side of the track about 1,200 feet from the point of impact. (See figure 3.) The tractor and semitrailer separated, the tractor rotating clockwise about 260 degrees and coming to rest about 19 feet southwest of the crossing. The semitrailer rotated counterclockwise about 285 degrees and came to rest about 43 feet southeast of the crossing. (See figure 4.) No fire ensued.

Emergency Response -- After the collision, the engineer got off the lead locomotive to assess damage to the train. He said he noted the milepost just beyond the derailed train and directed the assistant engineer to notify the CSXT dispatcher of the accident. According to the assistant engineer, he switched to the CSXT emergency channel, and within seconds the dispatcher responded. The assistant engineer said he relayed the train's location and indicated that his train needed help.

At 2:35 a.m., a resident nearby made a call to 911 reporting the accident. The caller stated that there had been a passenger train wreck about one mile north of Sycamore, that a train had hit a tractor-semitrailer crossing the tracks, and that there may be casualties. According to Allendale County Central Dispatch records, at 2:35 a.m., an Allendale County deputy sheriff was dispatched to the scene, arriving about 2:59 a.m. When the deputy sheriff arrived, he saw the truckdriver walking around unhurt, and he made minimal observations of the train. He told his dispatcher that the truckdriver was not hurt and that CSXT should be notified of the derailment. The deputy was asked by the dispatcher if emergency medical services (EMS) were needed, and he responded "negative."

At 3:05 a.m., a dispatched South Carolina Highway Patrol (SCHP) trooper arrived on the scene. He said he interviewed the deputy sheriff and the truckdriver, and when he saw white bedding sheets lying on the ballast, he concluded that there may be injured passengers aboard. He contacted the SCHP dispatcher, who, at 3:17 a.m., called the Allendale County dispatcher and requested an ambulance. At 3:25 a.m., the SCHP trooper asked the dispatcher to send the fire department with ladders to help passengers out of the overturned cars. Between 2:35 and 3:17 a.m., no EMS assistance was requested or dispatched.

The Allendale County Emergency Operations Plan was initiated at 3:43 a.m. by the first-arriving Allendale County paramedic. At 3:45 a.m., a paramedic supervisor established a command center at the accident site. Mutual aid was requested for ambulances and fire units from neighboring counties. Three area hospitals were alerted that they may receive patients from the train accident. Forty-seven persons were transported to the three hospitals. School buses were used to transport uninjured passengers to shelters. By 4:00 a.m., responders had evacuated all persons from train 81, and by 6:19 a.m. the last passenger had been transported to an area hospital. About 7:00 a.m., the Allendale County fire chief, who was the incident commander, turned the scene over to CSXT.

IMPACT POINT

Figure 3 -- Final rest position of train

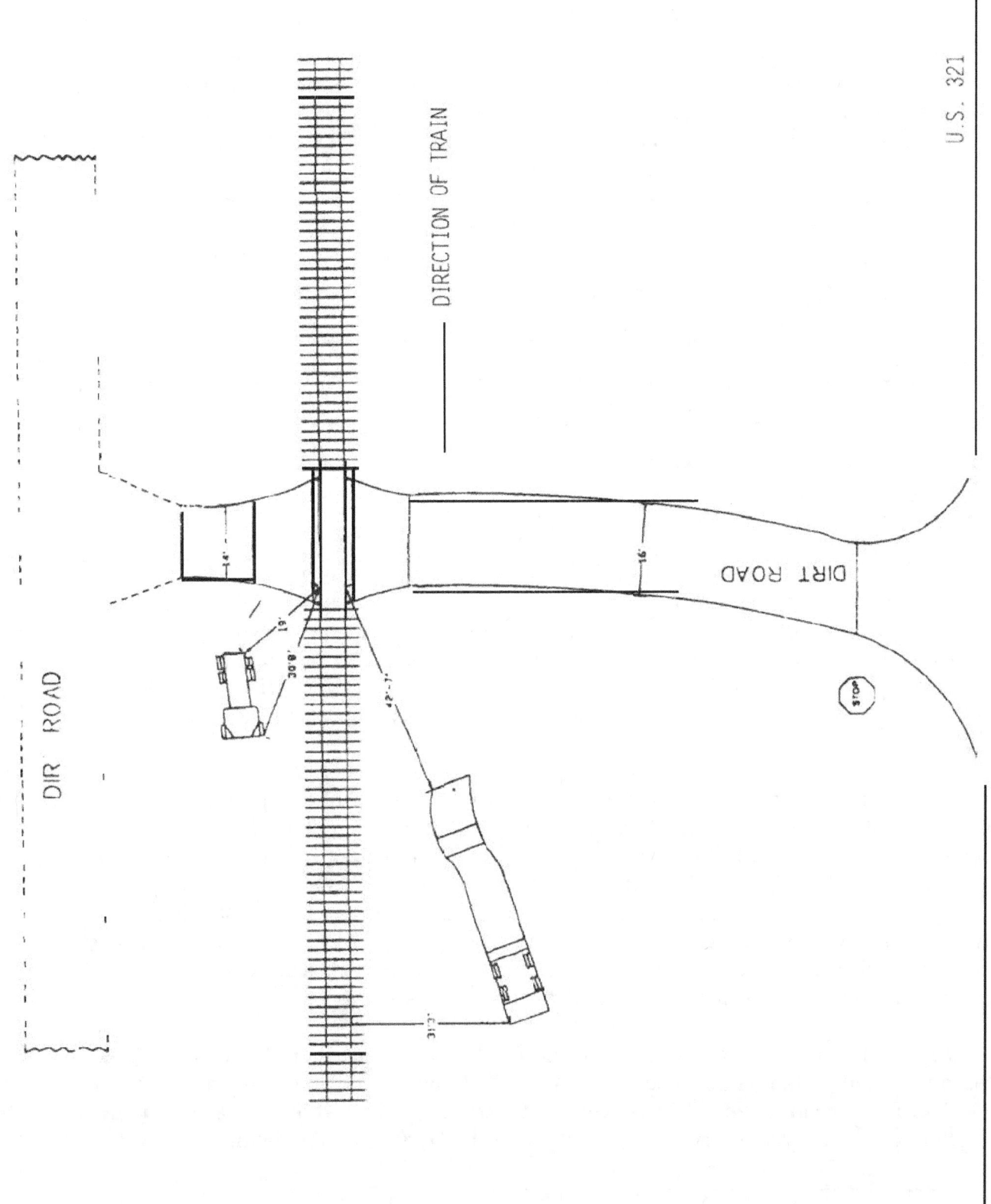

Figure 4 -- Final rest positions of tractor and semitrailer

Injuries

No fatalities or serious injuries resulted from this accident; however, 29 passengers and 4 OBS personnel sustained minor injuries. Most of the injured persons were located either in the coach or sleeper cars. Three passengers with preexisting conditions were admitted to area hospitals. The train operating crew and truckdriver were not injured. An injury table based on the Abbreviated Injury Scale (AIS) of the Association for the Advancement of Automotive Medicine is shown at appendix B.

Table 1 -- Injury table[3]

Injury Type	Operating Crew	Service Crew	Passengers	Others	Totals
Fatal	0	0	0	0	0
Serious	0	0	0	0	0
Minor	0	4	29	0	33
Total	0	4	29	0	33

Damage

The truck combination unit, both locomotives, three mail-handling cars, the sleeper car, both baggage cars, the lounge and dining cars, and six passenger coaches were damaged in the accident. About 690 feet of track were damaged or destroyed. O&J estimated repairs to the tractor and replacement cost for the semitrailer at $60,000. Amtrak estimated damage to the rolling stock at $1,018,500. CSXT estimated damage to the track at $50,000, with cleanup costing an additional $154,000. Total damage estimates for this accident thus were about $1,282,500.

Truck -- The tractor's engine compartment fiberglass cover tilted upward during the collision. The right steering axle tire, both left drive axle outside tires, and the right rear drive axle outside tire were deflated. Both frame rails were displaced to the left, causing the front and rear drive axles to be misaligned. The tractor cab protection rack separated from the tractor frame. During impact, the lowbed semitrailer separated from the tractor at the fifth wheel, with the fifth wheel remaining attached to the semitrailer. The right side of the semitrailer was bent inward to a maximum displacement of 40 inches. The left landing gear leg was bent rearward, and the right landing gear foot had rotated upward to a vertical position.

Train -- The lead locomotive sustained damage to its front plow and right-side ladder, and its rear truck derailed. The trailing locomotive derailed. No interior damage was noted in either locomotive. The three mail-handling cars behind the locomotives derailed but remained upright; the 4th through 7th cars derailed and overturned or tipped to varying degrees on their right sides;

---

[3]Table 1 is based on the injury criteria of the International Civil Aviation Organization, which the Safety Board uses in accident reports for all modes.

the 8th through 14th cars derailed but remained upright and parallel to the track; and the 15th and 16th cars remained on the rails. A post-impact inspection revealed that the emergency windows had been removed from the lounge and several coach cars; both automatic brake valves (controlling the train's brakes) on the lead locomotive were in the emergency position; the independent brake handle (controlling the locomotives' brakes) was in the fully applied position; the front headlights were on dim; and the ditch lights were off.

Truck Information

The truck consisted of a 1986 Freightliner 3-axle conventional tractor and a 1994 Evans two-axle semitrailer. The tractor was owned by O&J; the semitrailer was owned by Pioneer Machinery, Inc. (Pioneer). The tractor had a diesel engine coupled to an 11-speed manual transmission. At the time of the accident, the tractor's odometer registered 511,250 miles.

Lowbed or low clearance vehicles vary greatly in their physical characteristics, primarily because most trucks are customized for special operational conditions. Typical wheelbases for lowbed vehicles range from 25 to 40 feet, and ground clearances can be as little as 3 inches. The Pioneer semitrailer was approximately 48 feet long. It had an unloaded ground clearance of 12 inches on a level surface. All tractor and semitrailer axles were equipped with standard s-cam air mechanical service brakes. The truck had a overall length of approximately 61 feet. (See figure 5.)

A commercial inspection performed on the tractor in 1995 by the SCHP revealed several out-of-service violations. (See "Motor Carrier Information" section for details.) A postaccident examination of the semitrailer's landing gear revealed that it was partially retracted and was protruding about 3 inches below the bottom of the semitrailer. The landing gear was damaged during the impact sequence, but there was no evidence of preexisting problems. Lamps from both the tractor and semitrailer were removed and sent to the Safety Board's materials laboratory for further examination. (See "Tests and Research" section for findings.)

Train Information

Amtrak train 81, the Silver Star, was a regularly scheduled passenger train operating from New York City to Tampa, Florida. On the day of the accident, the train consisted of two locomotive units, three mail-handling cars, two baggage cars, one sleeper car, one slumber coach car, one Amlounge II car, one dining car, and seven coaches. The locomotive units were built by General Motors Electric-Motive Division and were equipped with 3,000-hp engines and 2-axle trucks. The locomotives were equipped with a 97-channel radio, airbrake equipment, and Pulse "dash 5" event recorders. The sleeper car was manufactured by Heritage, and the other 8 coach cars were Amtrak Amfleet II cars. (See table 2 for consist of train.)

9

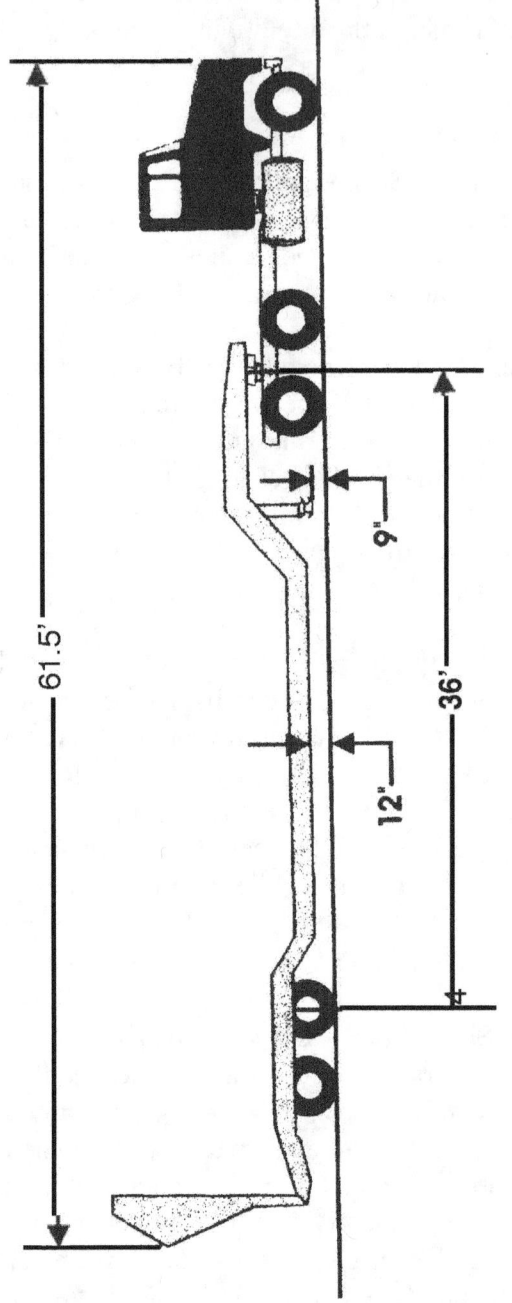

Figure 5-- Schematic of accident truck (not to scale)

61.5'

36'

12"

9"

Table 2 -- Train consist and estimated damages

Consist Position	Amtrak Car Number	Type	Usage	Postaccident Condition	Estimated Damage
,	372	Locomotive	PH 40	Damaged, rear truck derailed	$125,000
,	340	Locomotive	PH 40	Derailed	85,000
1	1567	Car	Mail Hand	Derailed	10,000
2	1425	Car	Mail Hand	Derailed, tipped	12,000
3	1471	Car	Mail Hand	Derailed, tipped	27,500
4	1268	Car	Baggage	Derailed, overturned	42,000
5	1135	Car	Baggage	Derailed, overturned	68,000
6	2457	Car	Sleeper	Derailed, overturned	270,000
7	25047	Car	Coach	Derailed, overturned	47,000
8	25020	Car	Coach	Derailed, tipped	100,000
9	25004	Car	Coach	Derailed, tipped	80,000
10	25029	Car	Coach	Derailed, tipped	45,000
11	28010	Car	Lounge	Derailed, tipped	60,000
12	8501	Car	Diner	Derailed	13,000
13	25040	Car	Coach	Derailed	18,000
14	25065	Car	Coach	Derailed	16,000
15	25068	Car	Coach	Unaffected	0
16	2088	Car	Coach	Unaffected	0
				Total	$1,018,500

Personnel Information

Truckdriver -- The truckdriver, age 40, had a valid South Carolina commercial driver's license (CDL). He said that he had driven trucks for about 14 years. He said he had driven various farm trucks, a sand dump truck, a cement truck, and an asphalt truck. He said he had also driven trucks with log semitrailers and wood chip semitrailers. He received his CDL in February 1992 after attending a CDL course.

The truckdriver's driving record indicated that since 1988 he had received six citations for speeding violations, one license suspension for failure to pay a ticket, and one suspension for driving without a valid license. He had been involved in three reported accidents during that period. Two of the citations were received and all three accidents occurred while the truckdriver was operating a commercial vehicle. He attended a defensive driving course after receiving points on his license for the above violations. In the 6-month period following this accident, the driver received two citations for speeding and one suspension for failure to pay a fine previously imposed for violations noted during a commercial vehicle inspection. Both speeding violations occurred while the driver was operating a commercial vehicle.

At the time of the accident, the truckdriver did not have a required medical certificate,[4] although he later obtained one. In February 1994, he was diagnosed with non-insulin-dependent diabetes. His condition was controlled by diet and with the medication Glynase.[5] He took one pill each day, and he did so on the morning of the accident. His personal physician stated during an interview with Safety Board investigators that he had not observed, nor had the driver complained of, any side effects from the medication. The driver was not asked to submit to a physical examination either for his CDL or as a condition of his employment with O&J.

The truckdriver had been regularly employed by O&J since March 1995, and had worked part time for the company since November 1994. The truckdriver stated that he was paid $.40 per mile, but only when his truck was loaded; he received no pay for driving without a load. Each week he supplied his employer with a work sheet showing the number of miles driven, where loads (usually logs) were obtained, where they were delivered, the weight of the loads, and delivery ticket numbers. Since the driver was not paid by the hour, neither he nor his employer kept records showing his number of on-duty hours each day.

The driver said he pulled his first lowbed semitrailer "about a year or two ago." He stated that, since that time, he has pulled lowbed semitrailers for several employers, including O&J, without ever becoming stuck. He said he had pulled the Pioneer-owned accident semitrailer several times previously, but not over the accident crossing. He said he was aware that it was longer and that it had different end ramps than the O&J semitrailers.

---

[4]A certificate required by Federal Motor Carrier Regulations (Section 391.45) acknowledging that the truckdriver is physically qualified to operate a commercial vehicle.

[5]Glynase is an orally administered blood-glucose-lowering drug.

The truckdriver acknowledged that he had occasionally gotten "bogged down" in the woods while pulling a semitrailer, but he said there had always been equipment and people available to assist him whenever help was needed. He said he had heard about lowbed semitrailers having difficulty traveling over grade crossings, but that he had not heard about any semitrailer actually becoming stuck on a crossing.

Because of the varied locations of his work assignments, the truckdriver said he brought the truck home after work 2 to 3 times a week and parked it in front of his brother's house where it would be secure. He stated that he had driven over the same crossing on other occasions without difficulty, whether pulling a log semitrailer or the lowbed semitrailer leased to O&J, both of which had higher ground clearances than the accident semitrailer.

The truckdriver was off duty on April 29 and 30. On May 1, he said he awoke between 6 and 6:30 a.m., and reported for work at 7:00 a.m. At the time of the accident, he had been awake 20 hours and on duty about 19 1/2 hours. He reported that he had not experienced any mechanical problems with the truck while on duty. Based on his statement regarding the time and distance he traveled on his way home, the Safety Board estimated that the driver had rested about 1/2 hour in Neeses while en route to Sycamore.

Traincrew -- The train 81 operating crew consisted of an engineer, an assistant engineer, a conductor, and two assistant conductors. The OBS crew consisted of an on-board crew chief and 8 crewmembers. Amtrak personnel records indicated that each operating crew member was qualified to operate on the CSXT Jacksonville Division.

The operating crewmembers were based in Jacksonville, Florida. The crew had worked on northbound train 82, arriving on schedule in Southern Pines, North Carolina, on May 1 at 4:35 a.m. They reported for duty on southbound train 81 at 9:33 p.m. on May 1 and boarded the train for the return trip to Florida at about 10:00 p.m. The engineer and assistant engineer were in the operating compartment.

Engineer -- The engineer was promoted to engineer in March 1975 and was hired by Amtrak on March 11, 1987. His most recent physical examination had been on August 26, 1994, and he stated that he was in good health. He wore glasses and was wearing them at the time of the accident. His engineer's certification was issued on April 15, 1994, with an expiration date of April 15, 1997. He had passed his most recent rules examination on October 24, 1994.

Assistant Engineer -- The assistant engineer was promoted to engineer on July 17, 1978, and was hired by Amtrak on December 21, 1988. His most recent physical examination had been on April 27, 1995. He indicated that he was in good health. His engineer's certification was issued on March 9, 1994, with an expiration date of March 9, 1997. He had passed his most recent rules examination on April 27, 1995.

Conductor and Assistant Conductors -- The conductor was hired on August 20, 1986. His most recent physical examination had been on May 4, 1993, and his most recent rules examination on April 27, 1995. One assistant conductor, who was hired on August 20, 1986, had

had his most recent physical examination on April 28, 1993, and had taken his most recent rules examination on April 21, 1995. The other assistant conductor was hired on May 2, 1987, had had his most recent physical examination on September 1, 1994, and had taken his most recent rules examination on April 27, 1995.

Toxicological Testing

The truckdriver was not tested for alcohol or illegal drugs. Federal Highway Administration (FHWA) regulations requiring postaccident drug and alcohol testing (49 CFR 382.303) did not apply in this case, since the accident did not result in a death or a citation. Nevertheless, Safety Board investigators telephoned the Allendale County Sheriff's Department and requested that the truckdriver be asked to voluntarily submit blood and urine specimens for postaccident testing. That request never reached the investigating officer; however, the investigating officer, who knew the driver, interviewed the driver some 35 to 40 minutes after the accident. He said that he had detected no odor of alcohol and that, while the driver acted nervous and very concerned, he did not display any behavior that would lead the officer to suspect that he was impaired.

Amtrak did not have the train's operating crew toxicologically tested after the accident, because 49 *Code of Federal Regulations* (CFR) 219.201(b) provides as an exception that "no [toxicological] test shall be required in the case of a collision between railroad rolling stock and a motor vehicle or other highway conveyance at a rail/highway grade crossing."

Accident Site Information

Roadway and Grade Crossing -- The accident grade crossing was located on an unnamed, unpaved roadway known to locals as Boogaloo Road. The road provided access across the CSXT right-of-way and extended from U.S. 321 westward to an unpaved county road. It varied from 10 to 16 feet in width, and was open to the public. Beginning at the west edge of U.S. 321, the road's westbound approach to the track had a slight vertical sag before ascending toward the crossing. The eastbound approach also ascended toward the track. The 111-foot-long westbound approach to the east rail had an average ascending grade of 5.28 percent. At 30 feet out from the east rail, the approach had a rise of 2.87 feet, for an average ascending grade of 9.97 percent. The 30-foot-long eastbound approach to the west rail had a rise of 1.06 feet, for an average ascending grade of 3.5 percent.

No speed limit signs were posted on the roadway. A stop sign was located on the eastbound approach of Boogaloo road at the U.S. 321 intersection. There were no pavement markings at the crossing approaches. There were no signs warning motorists driving low-ground-clearance vehicles of the hump crossing, nor were such signs required.

The grade crossing road surface was constructed of asphalt and crossing planks. A 4-inch-thick by 10-inch-wide crossing plank lay on each side of the rails, with asphalt material in the center of the track and on the outside of the rails extending 15 feet beyond the crossing plank.

14

The CSXT right-of-way generally extends 50 feet to either side of the main track centerline. The crossing was re-tied and resurfaced by CSXT in February 1993.

The U.S. Department of Transportation/Association of American Railroads (DOT/AAR) National Rail/Highway Crossing Inventory designates the Boogaloo Road grade crossing as 634810U. The crossing has been listed in the DOT/AAR inventory since the mid-1970s as a public crossing.[6] However, the county engineer for Allendale County stated that he was not aware that the east-west trafficway known as Boogaloo Road had ever been considered or maintained as a County roadway. Safety Board investigators researched county documents and found neither records relating to this roadway nor right-of-way agreements relating to the crossing. While the DOT/AAR inventory showed an estimated average daily traffic count of 25 vehicles at the Boogaloo Road grade crossing, neither Allendale County nor the South Carolina Department of Transportation (SCDOT) had traffic count data for the crossing, nor did the South Carolina Department of Public Safety have accident records for Boogaloo Road.

A postaccident examination of the roadway revealed two tire marks just west of the track. The marks were characteristic of tire marks produced by forcible lateral movement. The tire marks extended about 4 1/2 feet west of the track. Another tire mark extended about 16 1/2 feet west of the track in the north portion of the roadway. From that tire point, the arc-like tire mark extended in the southeast direction across the roadway.

About 1/2 mile south of the accident crossing was another passive grade crossing, and about 1 mile south of the accident crossing was a crossing with active warning devices[7] installed. About 1/2 mile north of the accident crossing was another passive grade crossing. All of these crossings were on the same CSXT main line, but only the Boogaloo Road crossing was a hump crossing.

The American Association of State Highway and Transportation Officials (AASHTO) has published standards for roadway vertical profiles at railroad/highway grade crossings that are applicable to newly constructed crossings. These standards and guidelines are discussed in the Other Information section of this report under "Hump Crossings." The Safety Board is not aware of any standards that are applicable to existing crossings.

Track, Wayside, and Crossing Signals -- The grade crossing was located at railroad mile post 429.6 on the Columbia Subdivision of the CSXT Jacksonville Division. CSXT had maintained the track to meet or exceed Class 4 Federal Railroad Administration (FRA) track safety standards. Passenger trains were authorized to operate over this line at a maximum speed of 79 mph.

---

[6]A location open to public travel where railroad tracks cross a road that is under the jurisdiction and maintenance of a public authority, as defined in Rail-highway Crossing Accident/Incident and Inventory Bulletin No. 14, U.S. Department of Transportation, Federal Railroad Administration, p. A-4.

[7]A warning system comprising gates, flashing lights, highway signals, wigwags, and/or bells and activated automatically by an approaching train.

In the accident area, the track was constructed of continuous welded rail. The rails lay on 14-inch double shouldered tie plates, which lay on 7-inch by 9-inch creosote-treated timber crossties 8 feet 6 inches in length. The ties rested on 12 inches of number 4 crushed granite stone.

The accident grade crossing had reflectorized railroad crossing (crossbuck) signs at each approach to the crossing. There were no railroad advance warning signs in place on Boogaloo Road, on U.S. 321, or on the adjacent county road.

Carrier Information

O&J Gordon Trucking -- O&J was owned and operated by Mr. and Mrs. (Orin and Justine) Gordon. O&J owned two tractors and leased three semitrailers, including one lowbed semitrailer. The company had operated as a for-hire carrier of logs, wood chips, and logging machinery and related equipment since 1990. Mr. Gordon, who had a valid medical certificate, said that he regularly drove one of the company's tractors and that the accident driver had driven the other since November 1994. O&J usually confined its motor carrier operations to a 100-mile radius of its principal place of business. Mr. Gordon reported that he performed the majority of inspection and maintenance operations on the O&J vehicles, and he had inspection and maintenance records for the accident tractor available at the company's office.

Mr. Gordon had known the truckdriver for several years, and had previously worked with him at Gordon Logging Company. He said he was aware of the driver's medical condition, but he did not attempt to determine if the driver had a valid medical certificate at the time he was hired. Mr. Gordon said he had briefly discussed the operating limitations of the Pioneer semitrailer with the accident driver before the accident. He also said the driver had been given a credit card to use for fuel, and he stated his belief that if the accident driver's vehicle ever became disabled, the driver would not call for a tow truck without first contacting Mr. Gordon for approval.

At the time of the accident, O&J was performing contract work for Pioneer, which had a main office in Lexington and a branch office in Walterboro. Pioneer officials in Walterboro reported that O&J performed occasional transportation services for the company as a motor carrier for hire, using Pioneer's lowbed semitrailer to transport Pioneer logging machinery and equipment to the company's customers between Walterboro and Lexington.

The accident driver and motor carrier engaged in interstate and intrastate commerce and were therefore subject to both Federal and State motor carrier safety regulations. As a motor carrier engaged in interstate commerce, O&J was subject to the Federal Motor Carrier Safety Regulations[8] (FMCSR), to include:

Section 391.45, requiring that drivers be medically examined and certified as physically qualified to operate a commercial motor vehicle;

---

[8]Title 49 CFR Parts 390-399.

Section 391.51, requiring that an employing motor carrier retain a qualification file at the motor carrier's principal place of business for each driver used;

Section 395.3, prohibiting a motor carrier from requiring or permitting a driver to drive

,more than 10 hours since his last 8 or more hours off duty,
,after having been on duty 15 hours since his last 8 or more hours off duty, or
,after having been on duty more than 60 hours in the last seven consecutive days; and

Section 385.8, requiring a motor carrier to ensure that its drivers prepare and submit a record of duty status. Section 395.1(e) exempts from this requirement drivers used within a 100-air-mile radius of the normal work reporting location if

,the driver's tour of duty does not exceed 12 hours followed by a minimum of 8 consecutive hours off duty,
,the driver does not drive more than 10 hours during any 12-hour duty tour, and
,the motor carrier retains records for 6 months showing the time each day the driver reported for work, the time the driver was released from work, and total number of hours the driver was on duty each day.

O&J was the subject of a U.S. Department of Transportation safety review in June 1993, which resulted in the assignment of a "satisfactory" compliance rating[9]. As a result of this accident, on May 5, 1995, the FHWA's Office of Motor Carriers, in cooperation with the State of South Carolina, conducted a compliance review of O&J's motor carrier operations. This review disclosed several violations of the FMCSR, including failure to use properly qualified drivers, failure to subject all drivers to appropriate drug testing, failure to keep accurate records of driver duty status and vehicle maintenance and inspections, and failure to ensure that vehicles were systematically maintained and repaired. As a result, O&J was given a rating of "unsatisfactory."

South Carolina has adopted the FMCSR and, with the exception of the insurance requirements[10] and the hours-of-service regulations, has made the regulations applicable to intrastate motor carriers. South Carolina code was amended to prohibit South Carolina intrastate commercial vehicle operators from driving:

,more than 12 hours following 8 consecutive hours off duty;
,for any period after having been on duty 16 hours following 8 consecutive hours off duty;
,after having been on duty 70 hours in 7 consecutive days; or
,more than 80 hours in eight consecutive days.

---

[9]See 49 CFR Part 385.
[10]See 49 CFR Part 387.

17

On April 3, 1995, while on a trip for O&J from Savannah, Georgia, to Estill, South Carolina, the accident driver and a different tractor-semitrailer combination were the subject of a South Carolina Department of Public Safety driver-vehicle examination that disclosed numerous vehicle violations, to include inoperative horn, turn signals, stop lamps, and side marker lamps; oil leaks from the engine and power steering unit; cracks in the frame crossmembers and fifth wheel; and chaffed or leaking brake system air lines. As a result, the vehicle was placed out of service, and the driver was issued a citation for violations of South Carolina's vehicle code.

CSXT Operations -- The single-track CSXT main line that passes through Sycamore carried approximately two freight trains and two scheduled Amtrak trains each day, and nearby residents would have been aware that those trains often ran during the night. CSXT employed a centralized traffic control signal system to control train movements over this track. Train 81 approached the accident crossing operating on a clear signal, indicating there was no rail traffic in the block and that all switches were properly lined. The train was authorized to proceed at the maximum speed of 79 mph.

While operating on CSXT track, Amtrak crews were subject both to Amtrak's *Manual of Instruction for Transportation Department Employees* and CSXT's operating rules, timetable, and practices. The CSXT timetable in effect for the Jacksonville Division on the day of the accident imposed no special restrictions in the area of milepost 429.6.

Amtrak Operations -- Amtrak operates approximately 200 passenger trains daily across the United States. Each day, six Amtrak trains (three northbound and three southbound) operate on the Washington-to-Florida routes.

Amtrak's annual ridership is about 22 million passengers. Annual ridership figures for Amtrak's major corridors are as follows:

- Northeast Corridor (NEC):   10.5 million
- Washington, D.C.-Florida: 0.8 million
- Santa Barbara-L.A.-San Diego: 1.5 million
- New York City-Buffalo (Empire):0.9 million

Amtrak speeds generally are limited to 79 mph on most of its operating territory, with the exception of the Northeast and Empire corridors. Trains can operate at speeds up to 110 mph on the Empire Corridor and up to 125 mph (the Metroliner) on the Northeast Corridor.

The total number of private grade crossings on Amtrak routes could not readily be determined using data available either from the DOT/AAR inventory or from Amtrak sources. A recent report on high-speed passenger operations[11] offers some information on the number of grade crossings on Amtrak routes between Washington, D.C., and Florida; however, the information may not reflect every private crossing. This report indicates that on the Washington to Richmond

---

[11]See *High Speed Passenger Trains in Freight Railroad Corridors: Operations and Safety Considerations*, Report No. DOT/FRA/ORD-95/05, issued December 1994.

segment there are 64 grade crossings (0.59 grade crossings per route mile); on the Raleigh to Charlotte segment there are 260 grade crossings (1.5 per route mile); and on the West Palm Beach to Miami segment, there are 73 grade crossings (1.03 per route mile). This compares to zero grade crossings on the Northeast Corridor and 37 grade crossings (0.22 grade crossings per route mile) on the Empire Corridor. This report also calculates that motor vehicle-train collisions occur at rail/highway grade crossings at a rate of about one in every 6.3 million train crossings.

CSXT representatives said their records showed a total of 202 grade crossings on the CSXT main line through South Carolina, including 90 crossings with active warning devices and 112 with passive devices. These records also indicate a total of 50 private grade crossings on this main line.

Train 81 was a regularly scheduled Amtrak revenue run originating daily from New York City with a final destination of Tampa, Florida. Amtrak operating crews receive special notices, bulletins, or messages about events that affect the movement of their train, but the crew of train 81 on May 2, 1995, did not receive any special notices regarding the area near milepost 429.6.

Meteorological Information

Allendale County police officials who arrived on the scene the morning of the accident reported that the weather was mild and dry, and skies were overcast. Although there was no ambient lighting, visibility along the track was unrestricted.

An Allendale County police official reported that the weather conditions during the Safety Board tests on May 3, 1995, were similar to the conditions at the time of the accident, with no ambient lighting and no visibility-limiting conditions present.

Survival Aspects

Forty-seven train occupants were taken to three area hospitals for possible treatment. Three passengers with preexisting illnesses,an 89-year-old passenger with pneumonia, a 51-year-old passenger with asthma, and an 82-year old passenger with chronic anemia,were admitted to local hospitals.

Twenty-nine passengers and four OBS crewmembers were treated for minor injuries such as muscle strains, contusions, and abrasions. All 33 of the injured were treated by hospital emergency room staff and released.

The Safety Board sent written surveys to the 47 train occupants who were taken to local hospitals. The surveys asked these individuals to recollect events shortly before and after the accident. Of those receiving the survey, 13 responded. Most of them stated that they were sleeping when the cars derailed and that they were awakened either by the jolt of the impact or by the sound of the cars derailing. The majority of the responding passengers stated they were injured when they were thrown out of their seats and struck other seats, the floor, the wall, or interior furnishings. Respondents stated that the traincrew and emergency response personnel assisted passengers in getting off the train, walking to the buses, locating personal belongings, and finding temporary shelter.

The chief deputy for the Allendale County Sheriff's Department said that his department had a longstanding, though unwritten, policy regarding incidents such as the Sycamore accident. He said the policy required deputies to call for emergency personnel, without hesitation, in the event of a train derailment. He said this policy was in effect at the time of the Sycamore accident, but he acknowledged that the deputy who responded to the accident did not make the appropriate determination in a timely manner.

Tests and Research

Locomotive Event Recorders -- The lead and trailing locomotives were equipped with Pulse MTR 48H8C-5 event recorders. Investigators found the seal on the lead locomotive's event recorder cut and lying on the machine. A CSXT road foreman told Safety Board investigators that he had inadvertently broken the seal but that he had not disturbed the media. The seal on the event recorder for the trailing locomotive was removed under the Safety Board's supervision in the presence of representatives from the FRA, Amtrak, and CSXT. Both tapes were removed and sent to the Safety Board's Vehicle Performance Division laboratory in Washington, D.C., for readout and evaluation. Although the trailing locomotive derailed, the axle generator for the event recorder was located on the lead locomotive front truck, which remained on the tracks.

Laboratory personnel determined from the event recorder that the lead locomotive throttle was at position 8 (the maximum) and that the train was traveling between 80 to 81 mph when the brakes were placed into emergency. FRA regulations at 49 CFR 229. 117(1) require that a locomotive built since December 31, 1980, be equipped with a speed indicator that is accurate to within ± 3 mph for speeds of 10-30 mph and ± 5 mph for speeds in excess of 30 mph. The assistant engineer stated that he and the engineer had checked the locomotive speed indicator against a trackside defect detector while en route to Sycamore and had noted that the locomotive speed indicator reading was 2 mph faster than the defect detector reading.

Laboratory personnel were able to determine from the event recorder tapes that the train traveled a minimum of 1,651 feet and a maximum of 2,229 feet during the 26 seconds that elapsed from the time emergency braking was first applied until the train came to a complete stop.

Train Stopping Distance -- Safety Board investigators calculated the distance within which a train configured similar to train 81 and traveling between 79 and 81 mph could reasonably be expected to stop. The calculations, based on a train length of 1,388 feet and a brake pipe[12] length of 1,504 feet, indicated that the braking deceleration rate would likely be about 4.08 feet per second^2 with a stopping distance between 2,015 and 2,111 feet ± 15 percent.

---

[12]*Brake pipe* refers to the compressed-air line that extends from the locomotive, through each car, to the end of the train. The engineer applies and releases the train's brakes by varying air pressure in the brake pipe.

Track--The track was checked for level, gauge, and line, and all were within the required standards for FRA class 4 track.

Additional Train Tests -- At the request of the Safety Board, the FRA performed air-brake system and safety-device testing on the train. No air leakage was observed on the locomotives or on the four undamaged passenger cars. Because of extensive damage to the brake systems on the remaining passenger, baggage, and mail cars, no tests were performed on those cars. The emergency-channel radios were tested by the Safety Board, and no abnormalities were found.

Sight Distance -- Safety Board investigators conducted three on-site tests to determine the distance at which Amtrak operating personnel could detect the presence of a large object on the accident grade crossing. The tests were conducted at 3:00 a.m. on May 3, 1995. The locomotive's headlights were illuminated on bright, and its ditch lights were oscillating on both sides. A tractor-lowbed semitrailer combination similar to the accident vehicle (the test lowbed semitrailer was yellow; the accident semitrailer was dark green) was parked on the grade crossing. The tractor headlights and hazard warning flashers were turned off.

In the first test, the locomotive was backed northward from the crossing. At a distance of 1,479 feet from the crossing, the test engineer could see the test vehicle, but he could not identify it as a truck.

In the second test, the locomotive was moved further northward. At a distance of 1,953 feet from the crossing, the locomotive was at the bottom of a 1-percent grade, and the test engineer could not see the test vehicle at all.

In the third test, the locomotive was moved southward toward the crossing to determine the distance at which the engineer could see a person waving his arms. That distance proved to be 686 feet.

Truck Lamp Examination -- Accounts differed regarding the lights on the accident truck. The truckdriver stated that the truck headlights were on and the four-way warning flashers were activated while he was attempting to dislodge the vehicle. The driver's cousin corroborated the driver's statement regarding the headlights, but he said he did not see the four-way flashers activated. The train operating crew said they saw no lights at all on the accident vehicle; however, because of the truck's orientation over the crossing, the lights may not have been visible to the traincrew in any case.

Because of the varying accounts, Safety Board investigators decided to examine the lights on the accident truck in an attempt to determine if they had, in fact, been turned on at the time of impact. Three headlights and four tail lamps/warning flashers were removed from the accident tractor, and five amber side marker lamps were removed from the accident semitrailer. All were examined by the Safety Board's materials laboratory. The examinations disclosed that although the filaments in some of the side marker lamps were broken, none of them showed any evidence of the hot stretching or deformation that typically occurs when illuminated lamps are subjected to impact forces. Although not conclusive, these examinations suggested that the side marker lights on the accident semitrailer were not illuminated at the time of the collision.

Emergency Notification Time -- The Safety Board reconstructed the time required for a citizen in Allendale County to advise the appropriate CSXT officials, through the local emergency response agency, of a stalled/lodged vehicle on CSXT tracks. Based on transcript records of Allendale County Central Dispatch, it typically takes less than 1 minute for the 911 operator to transfer a caller to Allendale County Central Dispatch. The Allendale County dispatcher, having appropriate telephone numbers to reach CSXT, should be able to reach the railroad within 2 minutes. Thus, the total time required for a typical call to reach the appropriate CSXT officials was estimated to be no more than 3 minutes.

The Safety Board also contacted CSXT officials regarding the average time it would take a CSXT dispatcher, after being notified of a stalled/lodged vehicle on the tracks, to contact a train operating crew and have them stop their train. They advised that, on average, it would take about 1 minute to reach the crew and instruct them to stop the train. Consequently, the total time needed for a 911 call to reach CSXT officials and for those officials to stop a train was estimated to be no more than 3 to 4 minutes.

Other Information

The Safety Board has had a longstanding objective of improving safety at highway/rail grade crossings. Since 1976, the Safety Board has investigated more than 300 grade crossing accidents and has focused on the many safety issues involved at intersections where the paths of motor vehicles and trains meet. The Board has issued some 190 safety recommendations to Federal and State agencies, railroads, and safety organizations in an effort to have deficiencies corrected. Although the number of accidents and deaths at grade crossings has been reduced dramatically, grade crossing accidents continue to be the largest single source of fatalities and injuries involving railroad operations.

Hump Crossings -- Safety Board investigators searched FRA accident data bases to determine how frequently accidents like the Sycamore accident occur nationwide. The FRA grade crossing accident/incident data base contains information on about 65,000 impacts between trains and highway vehicles that occurred during the 10-year period from 1984 through 1994.

Although the FRA accident data base does not specifically indicate which of these accidents occurred at hump crossings, possible hump crossing accidents include those accidents in which (1) a truck or truck-trailer was stopped or stalled on a grade crossing, (2) the driver was not in the vehicle, and (3) the vehicle was struck by a train.

Safety Board investigators searched the FRA data base and found that about 1,900 of the crashes that occurred between 1984 and 1994 met the aforementioned criteria. Of those accidents, 36 involved a derailment, 56 involved at least one injury, and 8 involved at least one fatality. Amtrak was involved in 141 of these accidents. Of these 141 accidents, 11 involved derailments, 4 resulted in at least one injury, and 2 involved at least one fatality.

Since 1983, the Board has investigated at least 16 accidents in which lowbed vehicles lodged on grade crossings and were struck by trains. (See appendix E for a detailed summary of each case.) Two of those 16 accidents occurred during the investigation and report preparation process for this accident. The 16 accidents, all of them non-fatal, resulted in 296 injuries and more than $19 million in property damage. (See table 3.)

Table 3 -- Lowbed vehicle/train collisions investigated by the Safety Board

CASE	DATE	LOCATION	TRAIN TYPE Freight (F) Passenger (P)	DEATHS	REPORTED INJURIES	ESTIMATED PROPERTY DAMAGE
1	8/25/83	Rowland, NC	P	0	29	$623,399
2	11/30/83	Citra, FL	P	0	59	200,119
3	9/4/85	Schriever, LA	P	0	0	40,000
4	10/30/86	Gary, IN	P	0	32	110,000
5	11/12/86	College Park, GA	F	0	0	90,000
6	12/22/86	Winlock, WA	P	0	3	252,000
7	1/15/87	Canby, OR	P	0	1	49,022
8	11/12/87	Halifax, NC	F	0	0	266,130
9	11/25/87	Seffner, FL	P	0	17	336,349
10	10/3/90	Encinitas, CA	P	0	13	285,000
11	5/11/92	East Patchogue, NY	P	0	28	173,837
12	6/30/92	Orange Park, FL	F	0	0	169,000
13	11/30/93	Intercession City, FL	P	0	59	14,000,000
14	5/2/95	Sycamore, SC	P	0	33	1,000,000
15	5/10/95	Graysville, GA	F	0	1	1,000,000
16	10/3/95	Devon, CT	P	0	21	500,000
				TOTAL	**296**	**$19,094,856**

Relevant information drawn from these 16 accident investigations is summarized below:

- At none of the accident crossings were signs posted warning operators of lowbed vehicles of the hazard of becoming lodged on the crossing.

23

- Four of the cases (5, 8, 12, and 15) involved freight trains; the remaining 12 cases involved passenger trains.

- Ten of the accidents occurred in states that required operators of certain lowbed vehicles to provide advance notification to the railroad of their intent to travel over a grade crossing. The laws in those states were similar or identical to section 11-703 of the *Uniform Vehicle Code and Model Traffic Ordinance* (Florida, cases 2, 9, 12, and 13; Indiana, case 4; Louisiana, case 3; North Carolina, cases 1 and 8; New York, case 11; and Washington, case 6[13]).

- In four cases, the truck was being operated in violation of laws or ordinances prohibiting the operation of that type vehicle over the crossing. In one case (case 1) the driver was attempting to bypass weighing stations because his gross vehicle weight exceeded that authorized by his permit. In two cases (cases 5 and 10) the drivers failed to heed signs prohibiting truck traffic over the crossing. In case 16, the truck was being operated off its permitted route.

- In only one case (case 13) was the crossing configured in substantial compliance with the AASHTO standard. (See "Standards and Guidelines" section below.) In all other cases, the tracks were at the high point of the crossing.

- The period of time that the lowbed vehicles were lodged on the tracks before being struck varied from 1 minute (case 9) to 35 minutes (the Sycamore accident, case 14). The average time the vehicles were lodged on the tracks before being struck was about 11 minutes.

- In 12 cases the truck operator did not attempt to contact either the police or the railroad before the collision. In six of these cases (3, 6, 7, 9, 11, and 16) the truck was lodged over the crossing for 5 minutes or less, and attempts to radio the train or change the signals in time to prevent the collision may not have been successful in any event. In the other 6 cases (1, 2, 4, 5, 8, and 14) the times the lowbed vehicles were lodged over the tracks ranged from a low of about 5 to 10 minutes (cases 1 and 8) to a high of 35 minutes (case 14), with an average time lodged over the crossing of about 15 minutes.

- In case 10, the police were notified via a 911 call that a vehicle was lodged over a grade crossing. The police agency was unable to find the toll-free number to call the railroad before the collision, which occurred three minutes after the 911 call. When the police did find the number, they got a busy signal on their first two attempts to telephone the railroad because the telephone line, which did not have a rollover feature, was busy with routine railroad communications.

---

[13]For more information on which States have this requirement, see *Collision of Amtrak Train No. 88 with Rountree Transport and Rigging, Inc., Vehicle on CSX Transportation, Inc., Railroad Near Intercession City, Florida, November 30, 1993* (NTSB/HAR-95/01).

- In case 12, one police agency notified the railroad of a blocked crossing in its jurisdiction. A second police agency in a neighboring jurisdiction then received another report of a blocked crossing via a 911 call, but the location the caller gave for the blocked crossing was incorrect. After checking crossings in its jurisdiction, the second police agency notified the railroad that all crossings in its jurisdiction were clear. The railroad then issued an all-clear signal to the train, which struck the lodged vehicle about 7 minutes later.

- In case 15, the police were on the scene within 1 minute of the vehicle's becoming lodged on the crossing. A passerby also called 911 and notified the authorities. Although the police reached the railroad before the collision, there was not enough time to stop the train.

Standards and Guidelines -- The American Railroad Engineering Association (AREA) guideline and the 1990 edition of the AASHTO standard for roadway vertical profiles at railroad/highway grade crossings state, in part:

> Acceptable geometrics necessary to prevent drivers of low-clearance vehicles from becoming caught on the tracks would provide the crossing surface at the same plane as the top of the rails for a distance of 2 ft. outside of the rails. The surface of the highway should also not be more than 3 in. higher nor 6 in. lower than the top of the nearest rail at a point 30 ft. from the rail unless track superelevation dictates otherwise . . . . [14]

Warning Signs -- In 1986, as a result of its study of grade crossing accidents,[15] the Safety Board issued Safety Recommendation R-86-50 asking the FHWA to require that warning signs be installed at hump crossings. The FHWA responded that, in its view, changes to the *Manual on Uniform Traffic Control Devices* (MUTCD) were not warranted at that time. Based on this response, the Safety Board classified the safety recommendation "Open--Unacceptable Action." In a 1988 study of 189 heavy truck accidents,[16] the Safety Board reiterated this recommendation, prompting the FHWA to respond that because problems remained with resolving when and where such signs should be placed, the recommended requirement would be "premature, if not infeasible." Based on this response, the Safety Board, on May 22, 1991, reclassified Safety Recommendation R-86-50 "Closed--Unacceptable Action."[17]

---

[14]*A Policy on Geometric Design of Highways and Streets*, American Association of State Highway and Transportation Officials (AASHTO), 1990, pp. 842-843, adopted as a Federal Highway Administration standard in April 1993 at 23 CFR 625.4.

[15]Safety Study--*Passenger/Commuter Train and Motor Vehicle Collisions at Grade Crossings (1985)* (NTSB/SS-86/04).

[16]Safety Study--*Case Summaries of 189 Heavy Truck Accident Investigations* (NTSB/SS-88/05).

[17]See appendix D for a summary of Safety Board recommendations and responses regarding collisions involving trains and lowbed semitrailers.

On June 12, 1995, the FHWA published a notice of proposed amendments (NPA) to the MUTCD requesting comments on, among other changes, a proposed warning sign for "substandard vertical profiles" at railroad crossings. Request II-120(c), "Standard Warning Signs for Substandard Vertical Profile at Railroad Crossings," stated that the MUTCD national committee proposed a new section entitled "Humped Crossings," which the FHWA further proposed be included in the next edition of the MUTCD. No diagram of the proposed sign was included in the NPA. Request II went on to state that the North Carolina Uniform Traffic Control Device Committee is developing a sign as well. When that sign is finished, the request said, the "FHWA will include both the text and the sign in a future notice of proposed rulemaking." The American Trucking Associations, Inc., (ATA) responded to the rulemaking and agreed with the "need for an appropriate sign." On September 15, 1995, the FHWA extended the comment period for this NPA to March 11, 1996.

The U.S. DOT *Railroad-Highway Grade Crossing Handbook* states:

> Drivers of low clearance vehicles can be warned regarding crossings that have a profile insufficient for a certain combination of wheelbase and underclearance. However, presently no nationally accepted criteria, procedures, or signing have been adopted to accomplish this.

Six states have been identified as having some form of hump crossing warning sign. Florida and North Carolina have installed signs throughout their respective states, but neither State has records that show the number of signs currently in place. There has been no evaluation by either State of the effectiveness of the signs. (See figure 6.)

U.S. DOT/AAR Inventory -- The DOT/AAR National Rail/Highway Crossing Inventory is a computerized data base designed to catalog all railroad public crossings, grade separations, private crossings, and pedestrian crossings throughout the country. The inventory consists of four data elements: Part I lists the geographic locations of the crossings; Part II provides information about public vehicular crossings and includes train movements; Part III contains physical data about each crossing; and Part IV, titled "Highway Department Information," addresses classifications and traffic volumes. Vertical alignment data on grade crossings is not included in any of the parts of the inventory, nor in any other data base known to the Safety Board.

The FRA is the custodian of the inventory data, which are kept current by updates received voluntarily from the States and railroads. The FRA has required that a systematic and uniform procedure be developed to assist it in processing the data. Under current updating procedures, individual states and railroads enter changes into a computer using a prescribed format. The 1994 *U. S. DOT Rail-Highway Crossing Safety Action Plan* in its summary states that "[a]ccess to valid data is key to good decision making." To meet that objective, the action plan recommended promoting "more systematic updating of the U.S. DOT/AAR National Highway-Rail Crossing Inventory."

Florida

North Carolina

New York (proposed)

New York (proposed)

Figure 6–Examples of advance warning signs for hump crossings.

Relationships Between Public Entities and Railroads -- Through its investigations and liaison activities with the parties responsible for grade crossings, the Safety Board has become aware that communication and coordination between and among those parties are often loosely defined and are in some instances almost nonexistent. Local public officials have complained that they are given no notice when track maintenance is performed at a grade crossing. Some have said that when notice is given, it is usually because the maintenance to be performed involves several crossings where closure may be required. A CSXT railroad official said in an interview with Safety Board investigators that the same lack of communication applies when local entities work on public right-of-way approaches to the carrier's tracks.

In December 1995, Safety Board investigators interviewed several traffic and highway engineers attending a DOT Grade Crossing Task Force meeting in Raleigh, North Carolina. The engineers were asked to comment on the extent of official railroad communication and cooperation with highway jurisdictions. The engineers advised the Safety Board that in cases of new construction projects involving considerable planning, funding, and work scheduling, they generally received excellent support and cooperation from railroad officials; however, for routine and general maintenance of grade crossings, communication and cooperation were usually inadequate. They said that railroad officials would sometimes notify them of upcoming maintenance, but that such notification would typically be in general terms with no specific information on locations, dates, and times. They said highway officials most often become aware of crossing maintenance work through complaints received from private citizens.

As noted previously, the Allendale County engineer indicated that he did not know if Boogaloo Road was a County road. After an unsuccessful search for a right-of-way agreement covering the accident crossing, the engineer acknowledged that, although no records were kept, occasionally the County had performed minor maintenance on the roadway. Shortly after the accident, CSXT barricaded the crossing approaches, in effect closing it to motor vehicle traffic. When questioned by a Safety Board investigator, CSXT officials stated that they had cleared the closure with DOT representatives in Columbia, South Carolina. The County engineer stated he was not consulted, but he expressed no concern that the crossing was closed. He added that his office had no agreement or other mechanism for establishing a relationship with the railroads that traversed Allendale County. The accident crossing was subsequently reopened.

The U.S. DOT *Railroad/Highway Grade Crossing Handbook* addresses situations like this in its chapter on "Identifying of Alternatives." The book states:

> Proper liaison should be established between railroad and highway authorities so that plans and scheduling of work can be coordinated to avoid the planning or execution of work on either the highway or railroad that might adversely affect the grade line of the other.

and

The maintenance of track and highway should be coordinated between the railroad and the highway agency. In this manner, the crossing approach can be maintained to present a smooth transition to the crossing.

Emergency Notification -- The accident crossing had no signs that would inform the public of steps to take or phone numbers to call in the event of problems at the crossing. There was no indication of which railroad was responsible for the crossing, nor was there any unique name or number posted that would have made it possible for anyone reporting a problem to have readily identified this particular crossing to the operating railroad.

The absence of emergency information at grade crossings is a serious safety issue that the Safety Board addressed in its study on grade crossing safety. As a result of that study, the Safety Board issued Safety Recommendations R-86-48 and -55 to the FRA and the FHWA, respectively, asking that those agencies work together to develop and require the implementation in each state of a grade crossing emergency notification system similar in concept to the State of Texas' public and toll-free 1-800 system. (See appendix C for a more detailed discussion of the Texas system and the other systems highlighted below.)

These safety recommendations were classified "Closed--Acceptable Alternate Action," based on replies dated September 4, 1990, from the FRA and February 22, 1991, from the FHWA. The FRA replied that the agency had taken a number of actions addressing emergency notification systems similar to the Texas system. For example, the agency undertook a study of the Texas system and gave it a positive assessment.[18] The FRA indicated that it would take a proactive role in promoting the concept and stated that some States have adopted or were considering variations of the Texas system. The FRA indicated it would support these State initiatives to implement 1-800 systems. The FHWA replied that it had distributed the FRA's assessment of the Texas system to its field offices and State highway agencies. The FHWA indicated that it supported the concept and that it would work closely with the FRA to promote some form of public toll-free system.

In addition to the Texas system, the Safety Board reviewed toll-free emergency notification systems currently operating in two other states and Canada that permit the general public to report problems at grade crossings. Also, the Safety Board reviewed five domestic and two foreign railroads that have emergency notification systems in operation. The salient details of each of these systems are highlighted below:

Texas -- The Texas system applies to all highway/rail crossings that are equipped with train-activated warning devices and are located on State- or county-maintained roadways. The law requires that each such crossing be posted with signs indicating the crossing's unique DOT/AAA inventory number and providing a 1-800 number to be used to report problems at the crossing. Calls go to operators at the State's Department of Public Safety, who relay the information to the railroads, if appropriate. The system was designed to be a mechanism for reporting malfunctions of active crossing warning devices, but it has become an around-the-clock

---

[18]See *An Evaluation of the Texas 1-800 Program*, completed by Texas Transportation Institute and Richards and Associates for the Office of Safety, Federal Railroad Administration, June 1989.

clearinghouse for telephone messages relating to problems of any kind at grade crossings. Operators said they receive three or four calls daily reporting blocked crossings. While most of these involve trains blocking the crossing, some calls have reported blockages by highway vehicles. About 4,600 of the state's 18,000 grade crossings have the 1-800 number posted.

Delaware -- A 1988 agreement between the Delaware Department of Transportation and Consolidated Rail Corporation (Conrail) initiated a program whereby Conrail would establish and maintain a toll-free number posted at Conrail's public grade crossings and available for use by the public and local agencies to report problems at the crossings. Calls were to go to Conrail's communications and signals trouble desk in Columbus, Ohio. The program was funded by the State until 1993; since that time, the program has been funded by Conrail. Delaware transportation and railroad officials reported that they would like to reactivate the program at the State level and expand it to include the five other railroads operating in the state. Of the state's 451 public grade crossings, 183 (41 percent) have the 1-800 number posted.

Connecticut -- In 1990, Connecticut enacted a law requiring railroad companies operating trains that exceed 25 mph to erect emergency notification signs at all their grade crossings having gates or signals. The signs are to advise the public to use the 911 emergency number to report malfunctioning gates or signals. The 911 operator forwards reports to local police, who, in turn, notify the railroads. Each railroad company must report to the local municipality all actions taken as a result of these calls. About 150 (28 percent) of the state's 530 grade crossings have signs installed.

Canada -- Canadian National Railway Company developed and implemented an around-the-clock 1-800 emergency notification system in its Southern Ontario District in 1994. All public crossings, active and passive, within the district were posted with signs providing the emergency number and the crossing location. Calls go to railroad police, who relay the information as necessary. The Canadian National is undergoing a merging and reforming of its various districts, and railroad officials indicated that they expect all the new districts to move toward implementing the 1-800 system.

Norfolk Southern Corporation -- In 1994, the Norfolk Southern Corporation (NS) implemented a 1-800 Crossing Hotline program to facilitate notification of crossing signal malfunctions. The calls go to NS police, who relay the information to chief train dispatchers. NS officials reported that signs are in place at the 7,000 NS grade crossings where active warning devices are installed. Since the signs are intended primarily for use in reporting signal malfunctions, the company has not signed passive grade crossings. The company reported that the system in several instances has already been effective in safely stopping trains, and that the NS manager of grade crossing safety is studying the application of the program to passive crossing locations.

Santa Fe Railway Company -- The Santa Fe railroad established a 1-800 emergency telephone system in 1991. Officials reported that about 3,000 grade crossings are signed with the railroad's name, street address, milepost location, the DOT/AAR inventory number, and the 1-800-number. The signs are visible not only to the public, but to the crews of passing trains who may need to report problems at grade crossings. Calls go to railroad police. Santa Fe officials reported that they have averted some blocked-crossing accidents because of timely reports made using the system.

CSXT -- On July 12, 1995, Safety Board staff met with officials of CSXT who reported that the company is establishing a 1-800 emergency telephone number for public use. The telephone call-in system began operating in February 1996. CSXT representatives said they do not plan at this time to install appropriate signage at all crossing locations on their system, but they do plan to publicize the notification telephone number.

Other U.S. Railroads -- The Burlington Northern Railroad Company and the Union Pacific Railroad Company have 1-800 emergency notification systems that are available only to law enforcement and other public officials in the areas served by those railroads.

Foreign Railroads -- The French National Railway emergency notification system employs telephone call boxes installed at 9,400 (83 percent) of the country's 11,300 active grade crossings. The railroad reported that, while no logs are kept of the calls received by this system, there have been emergency trains stops made as a result of such calls.

The Japanese system for emergency notifications incorporates emergency buttons located at many of the country's grade crossings. The button is intended for use by motorists in the event a vehicle blocks a crossing. The button activates a wayside signal system that alerts train operators of a problem at the crossing.

Commercial Driver Training and Education -- As a result of its investigation of a 1983 collision of an Amtrak passenger train with a truck lodged on a hump crossing in Rowland, North Carolina,[19] the Safety Board issued Safety Recommendation H-84-66 asking that the FHWA issue an "On Guard" bulletin alerting motor carriers and warning truckdrivers of the hazards of driving over hump crossings. The FHWA complied with this recommendation in 1984 and again in 1989 when the Safety Board reiterated the recommendation as part of it efforts to highlight the continuing hazards of hump crossings.

A recent edition of the *Truckdriver's Handbook* published by the American Trucking Associations, Inc., includes the following:

> Railroad crossings with steep approaches can cause your unit to hang up on the tracks. The danger is greatest when using a single-axle tractor to pull a long semitrailer with the landing gear set back to accommodate a tandem tractor, or when pulling a low-slung semitrailer with limited ground clearance. If your truck does hang up on the tracks, immediately call the authorities, give the crossing location, and ask that the railroad be notified. (Page 27)

and:

---

[19]Railroad/Highway Accident Report--*Collision of Amtrak Train No. 88 with Tractor Lowboy Semitrailer Combination Truck, Rowland, North Carolina, August 25, 1983* (NTSB/RHR-84/01).

When driving equipment with low ground clearance, such as drop-frame or lowbed semitrailers, avoid places with changes in the grade of the road which may cause the unit to hang up in a dangerous place, cause damage, and require assistance to free the unit. (Page 29)

The Truck Trailer Manufacturer's Association (TTMA) also advised the Safety Board that it will issue a technical bulletin to its membership regarding hump grade crossings. The bulletin will include definitions for "lowboy" and "lowbed" semitrailers, suggest decal placement on low-ground-clearance semitrailers, and advise members as to what actions should be taken if a vehicle becomes lodged on railroad tracks.

The model *Commercial Driver License Manual* addresses grade crossing safety in Section 2.12, as well as the topic of hump crossings. This information, however, was taken, in severely abbreviated form, from the ATA *Truckdriver's Handbook*. Furthermore, none of the questions on the CDL test relate to grade crossing safety or specifically to the hazards of hump crossings.

Safety Board staff held a meeting on October 10, 1995, with industry representatives from the ATA, the Specialized Carriers and Rigging Association, the National Automobile Transporters Association, the TTMA, and Operation Lifesaver, Inc.[20] The purpose of the meeting was to discuss potential ways of informing truckdrivers of the hazards of hump crossings. The following was suggested by industry participants at the meeting:

- Truckdrivers can be alerted to the hazards of hump crossings, but no universal set of instructions can be developed to guide them through every crossing.

- Hump crossings should be identified and signed accordingly.

- Operation Lifesaver can, and will, be more proactive in addressing the hazards of hump crossings and low-ground-clearance vehicles in its truckdriver grade crossing safety education efforts for trucking groups.

- The hazards of hump crossings and recommended actions to take when a vehicle becomes lodged are currently addressed in at least two industry publications for truckdrivers. Such industry efforts will continue.

---

[20]Operation Lifesaver is an ongoing public education program designed to reduce the number of crashes, deaths, and injuries at highway-rail intersections. To meet its goals, the program strives to increase public awareness of the highway-rail crossing environment and to improve driver and pedestrian behavior at these intersections by encouraging observance of traffic laws relating to crossing signs and signals. Also, the program emphasizes the enforcement of existing traffic laws and promotes engineering improvements at grade crossings, to include installation and upgrade of warning devices and signs.

- The implementation of a 1-800 emergency telephone notification system at both passive and active-warning-device-controlled crossings would enhance the likelihood of railroads being warned of a blocked crossing.

Grade Crossing Safety -- Since 1974, according to the U.S. General Accounting Office, approximately $4.9 billion has been appropriated by Congress to address the improvement of grade crossings through the Rail-Highway Crossing Program (Section 130 of the Highway Safety Act of 1973). This program provides grant money to States that agree to conduct and maintain a survey of grade crossings that may require improvement, establish and implement a schedule of safety improvement projects, and undertake crossing improvements according to a State priority list.

For the period from fiscal year 1974 through fiscal year 1994, almost $3 billion in Federal funds was allocated for 29,500 grade-crossing-improvement projects. Most of the money, about 56 percent, has been used to install active warning devices at grade crossings. Other funds have been used for grade crossing separations, grade crossing eliminations, safety demonstration projects, or other purposes. In fiscal year 1995, about $149.5 million was appropriated for this program, according to the FRA.

The national responsibility for grade crossing safety is split within the U.S. DOT. Four agencies have responsibilities for grade crossing safety,the FRA, the FHWA, the National Highway Traffic Safety administration (NHTSA), and the Federal Transit Administration (FTA). At the State level, the responsibility for grade crossing safety is generally distributed throughout a variety of agencies, including State regulatory agencies and State transportation departments. Some states, for example, have public service or utility commissions that have this responsibility. In other states, some safety decisions are left up to local governments.

The U.S. DOT, recognizing that grade crossing safety needed a guiding document, issued the 1994 *Rail-Highway Crossing Safety Action Plan*, which included 55 proposals. Safety improvements for passenger or commuter train routes were not specifically targeted in this plan.

In October 1995, the Secretary of Transportation created a Grade Crossing Safety Task Force to conduct a review of national highway/rail grade crossing design and construction safety countermeasures. The task force, which was designed to complement the ongoing work of the action plan and to further DOT goals, addressed issues beyond the scope of the action plan. Through the task force, the DOT investigated and assessed the decision-making, coordination processes, and safety aspects pertaining to the planning, design, construction, maintenance, operation, and inspection of highway/rail grade crossings. The task force developed recommendations and submitted them to the DOT Secretary. Those recommendations were released to the public on March 4, 1996.

The task force evaluated problems in the following areas: interconnected (pre-empted) signals; storage; high-profile (hump) crossings; light rail transit crossings; and inclusion of grade crossing information in the permit process for slow, low, and special vehicles (including oversized and overweight vehicles whose routes take them over grade crossings).

ANALYSIS

General

In the following analysis, the Safety Board will identify those factors that created the accident scenario, exclude those factors that did not influence the accident outcome, and determine which factors did influence or contribute to the accident. Discussion will focus specifically on why the truckdriver became lodged on the grade crossing and why he took the actions he did after becoming lodged. Among the issues addressed will be driver fatigue, driver training and experience, and motor carrier involvement during the accident sequence of events. The actions of the truckdriver will be evaluated in the context of other, similar accidents the Safety Board has investigated. Finally, the analysis will address both short- and long-term measures that could be taken to prevent similar accidents in the future.

Exclusions

The Amtrak crew were qualified to perform their duties and were fit for duty. The traincrew were in compliance with the hours-of-service requirements, and the train was being operated in accordance with both CSXT and Amtrak operating practices. Safety Board investigators were able to exclude as factors contributing to this accident the condition of the track, the operation of the wayside signals, the mechanical condition of the train, and the weather.

Train 81 approached the accident crossing operating on a clear signal. According to event recorder data, the train traveled between 1,651 and 2,229 feet after emergency braking was applied. The Safety Board calculated the stopping distance for a train operating between 79 and 81 mph to be between 2,015 and 2,111 feet.

Although the event recorder data reflects, within a range, the actual stopping distance for train 81 during the accident, these distances are not representative of the stopping distance that would be expected in a non-accident situation. During the impact sequence, the train struck the semitrailer, which in turn caused the locomotives and 14 of the 16 cars to derail. The impact and the derailments created a significant drag on the train, reducing the stopping distance. Moreover, the event recorder data were generated based on a sampling rate of once every 2 to 3 seconds, which could have introduced some degree of error in the distances recorded for the 26-second braking sequence.

The braking distances calculated by the Safety Board, which were based on an industry-accepted formula derived for train brake engineering,[21] represent stopping distances required in a non-accident situation. Thus, the calculated stopping distances of 2,015 to 2,111 feet would be more appropriate than the distance shown by the event recorder for determining the distance the operating crew would have needed to stop in time to avoid the collision.

Safety Board investigators estimated that it would have taken a minimum of 1.5 to 2 seconds for the train assistant engineer to perceive the hazard and react by applying the train's emergency brakes. Thus, under optimum conditions, the assistant engineer would have had to have seen the truck or some other stimulus somewhere between 2,191 and 2,346 feet from the crossing in order to have had a chance to stop in time to avoid a collision.[22]

It should be pointed out, however, that in order to avoid injuries to passengers and unnecessary damage to rolling stock, passenger train engineers will not usually activate emergency braking at the first sign of a potential hazard; instead, they will wait until they have a reasonable certainty that the hazard is real, for example, that the truck is not going to move off the crossing. This delay could add several seconds to the optimum reaction time. In this accident, because of the low ambient light, brake application could have come as much as 4 seconds after the traincrew first saw the semitrailer. Consequently, when reaction time is considered, the traincrew would have needed between 2,484 and 2,580 feet[23] to perceive the semitrailer, realize it was a hazard, and bring the train to a stop short of the crossing.

The sight distance tests conducted by the Safety Board revealed that the track geometry made it impossible for the traincrew to see the crossing at night beyond about 1,953 feet. Further, though the test engineer could see something on the crossing at 1,479 feet, he could not distinguish it as a truck. Because both of these distances are substantially less than the minimum of 2,484 feet the Safety Board determined would be required for the traincrew to perceive, realize, and respond to the hazard, the Safety Board concludes that even if the train operating crew had seen the truck on the crossing at their first opportunity, they would not have had sufficient distance to stop the train and avoid the collision.

The above analysis is consistent with the traincrew's statements regarding sight distance to the accident crossing. During the accident sequence, the first indication the traincrew had of the hazard came at 1,335 feet from the crossing (near the whistle post) when they saw the driver running along the track waving his arms. Almost immediately they saw the lodged vehicle, but it was obviously too late at that point to avoid the collision.

---

[21]Braking formula from *Engineering and Design for Railway Brake Systems*, Air Brake Association, 1984 edition, p. II-16.

[22]At train speeds reported/recorded between 79 and 81 mph, averaging 80 mph:
 Best case stopping distance: 1.5 sec. x 80 mph (88/60) = 176 ft. + 2,015 ft., or 2,191 ft.
 Worst case stopping distance: 2.0 sec. x 80 mph (88/60) = 235 ft. + 2,111, or 2,346 ft.

[23]At train speeds reported/recorded between 79 and 81 mph, averaging 80 mph:
 Best case stopping distance: 4 sec. x 80 mph (88/60) = 469 ft. + 2,015 ft. + 2,484 ft.
 Worst case stopping distance: 4 sec. x 80 mph (88/60) = 469 ft. + 2,111, or 2,580 ft.

The truckdriver was qualified to operate the truck. He had a valid CDL and had operated commercial vehicles about 14 years and lowbed vehicles for 2 years. Although he engaged in interstate operations and was therefore subject to certain Federal and State motor carrier requirements, he did not have a medical certificate or maintain daily logs for all applicable trips. When the truck became lodged on the crossing, he had been on duty for about 19 1/2 hours, which exceeded the number of hours allowed under the Federal and State hours-of-service regulations. (The issue of truckdriver fatigue is discussed in more detail later in this analysis.)

On the other hand, even though the truckdriver did not have a medical certificate and was a non-insulin-dependent diabetic, his physical condition did not disqualify him from driving a commercial vehicle. In fact, he obtained a medical certificate shortly after this accident. The truckdriver was very familiar with the roadway, the grade crossing, and the equipment he was operating. It is therefore highly unlikely that, had the truckdriver been in conformance with the medical and driver log requirements, he would have done anything different to change the outcome of this accident.

The truckdriver indicated that he had not experienced any mechanical problems with the truck before the accident. Although several vehicle violations were noted in April 1995, none of those violations would have caused the truck to become lodged. Also, a post-impact inspection of the truck did not reveal any preexisting mechanical problems that would have caused the truck to stall or become inoperable on the railroad tracks. Physical evidence did indicate that the semitrailer's landing gear, which protruded some 3 inches below the semitrailer frame rails, became embedded in the asphalt surface at the crossing before impact occurred. Although the landing gear was damaged in the impact, there is no indication that it was defective or had malfunctioned.

No postaccident toxicological tests were performed on the truckdriver or traincrew. State and federal law did not require such testing under the circumstances surrounding this accident. On-scene observations by the responding emergency personnel of the behavior of the driver and traincrew after the accident did not suggest drug or alcohol use by any of the operators. Consequently, the Safety Board concludes that there is no evidence to indicate that either the truckdriver or Amtrak crewmembers were impaired by alcohol or other drugs.

The Accident

The accident truck became lodged because of the truck configuration and the accident crossing geometry. The longest span between the five axles of the accident truck was about 36 feet from the center of the tractor tandem axles to the center of the first axle on the semitrailer. The minimum ground clearance for the frame rails of the semitrailer was about 12 inches, and minimum ground clearance for the landing gear was about 9 inches.

The westbound approach to the crossing ascended to about a 10-percent grade. The AASHTO standard for roadway vertical profiles recommends that highway surfaces not exceed a 2-percent ascending grade 30 feet out from the rails, meaning that the accident crossing grade was almost 5 times over the recommended allowance. Taking into account this profile and the accident truck configuration, Safety Board investigators calculated that the semitrailer would have needed a minimum ground clearance of 16 inches to successfully negotiate the crossing.[24] Consequently, the semitrailer would have become lodged even if the landing gear had not first struck the crossing asphalt surface. Thus, the Safety Board concludes that the truck, as configured, could not safely travel over the crossing because of the crossing's substandard geometric characteristics.

Truckdriver Issues

Driver Fatigue -- It is possible that at the time of the accident the driver was fatigued from a lack of sleep, since he had been on duty for 19.5 hours and awake for about 20 hours. In order to assess whether fatigue influenced the driver's behavior before or after his truck became lodged on the crossing, Safety Board investigators examined the driver's sleep/wake cycle, as well as his training and experience.

In the Safety Board's recent Safety Study *Factors that Affect Fatigue in Heavy Truck Accidents* (NTSB/SS-95/01), three critical measures were identified as predictors of fatigue-related accidents. One of those measures,the amount of sleep a driver has obtained in the past 24 hours,suggests a potential for fatigue with this driver. The Safety Study found that drivers in fatigue-related accidents had had an average of 6.9 hours' sleep in the 24 hours preceding the accident. In comparison, the driver in this accident had had only 3.5 to 4 hours' sleep in the 24 hours before the accident, well below the Study's average. Such limited sleep and long hours suggest the driver may have been fatigued.

Moreover, the driver was operating at a time of night (about 2:00 a.m. when he got stuck) when he would normally have been asleep. This would have created some disruption in his personal circadian cycle, which could have led to fatigue. When these two aspects of the driver's sleep/wake cycle are taken in the aggregate, it appears likely that he was fatigued when the accident occurred.

Some indication of fatigue was also supplied by the driver himself. He reported that when he was not able to get the logging equipment started in Lexington, he wanted to go home and get some sleep. While en route home and within an hour of the accident, the driver stopped for a 30-minute nap in his truck, further suggesting that he was fatigued.

The Safety Board recognizes that the effects of fatigue range from relatively subtle impairment to overt incapacitation. Where this driver fell on that continuum before his nap is unknown. What is known is that napping can be an effective countermeasure to fatigue and can enhance alertness and improve performance. A recent National Aeronautics and Space Administration (NASA) study of the effectiveness of napping during flight operations[25] revealed

---

[24]The Safety Board used "HANGUP" software developed at West Virginia University (R. Eck and S. Kang) to simulate the movement of large trucks over grade crossings and to predict where hang-up problems will occur for low-ground-clearance vehicles.

[25]Rosekind, M.R., Gander, P.H., Connell, L.J., Co, E.L., *Crew Factors in Flight Operations X: Alertness Management in Flight Operations,* NASA Technical Memorandum (DOT/FAA/RD-93/18), December 1994, p. 45.

that naps of similar duration to the one this driver took were "demonstrated to be effective acute fatigue countermeasures." Consequently, although the driver may have been fatigued from a lack of sleep, it is likely that the driver suffered less from the effects of fatigue than would be implied by the number of hours he was awake.

Driver Training and Experience -- In order to further determine the role driver fatigue may have played in this accident, it was necessary for investigators to evaluate his behavior in light of his training and experience with respect to the compatibility of hump crossings and lowbed trailers. The driver had no formal training that addressed the compatibility of hump crossings and lowbed trailers; most of his knowledge came from on-the-job experiences. His employer reported that he had talked to the driver about the difficulties associated with operating lowbed trailers in logging areas and on highways. The employer advised the driver to find an alternate route if at any time he felt he may become stuck in the woods or on a grade crossing.

In this case, however, the driver was very familiar with the accident grade crossing and its humped profile, having lived near it much of his life. He had gone over the crossing without difficulty innumerable times before while driving a variety of vehicles. Not only had he never experienced a problem at this crossing, or any crossing, he was unaware that anyone else had ever become hung up on a grade crossing.

In the 5 months preceding the accident, while he was living with his father about 100 yards from the crossing, the driver had had occasion to drive the accident tractor and his regularly assigned log trailer over the crossing two to three times per week, to and from work, and had never experienced any difficulty. Moreover, he had traversed the crossing with his employer's lowbed trailer, which had a ground clearance of 24 3/4 inches, with no problems. He had not pulled the accident trailer over the accident crossing, but he had pulled it without difficulty over another crossing in Sycamore. Consequently, the driver's experience in traversing this and other grade crossings gave him no reason to be concerned about becoming lodged.

Unfortunately, the majority of the driver's experience involved pulling trailers significantly different,particularly in ground clearance,from the accident trailer. During the 3 months preceding the accident, he had pulled a lowbed trailer about 15 times. The lowbed trailer he usually pulled was the one leased to O&J, although he had also pulled the accident lowbed trailer 3 or 4 times previously. He was probably not aware of the fact that, because the accident lowbed trailer was longer and lower than the O&J trailer, it was much more susceptible to becoming lodged on hump crossings.

Another relevant aspect of the driver's experience concerns the physical environment in which he often operated lowbed trailers. The driver's job required that he pull a lowbed trailer only when he needed to deliver or pick up a logging vehicle at an off-road logging site. Such off-road locations, typically in the woods, greatly increase the likelihood that a truck will become stuck. In fact, the driver reported he had occasionally gotten "bogged down" in the woods, but there had always been equipment there to pull his truck/lowbed trailer clear of any obstruction. Again, like other parts of the driver's experience, the off-road aspect gave him little reason to be concerned about becoming lodged with a lowbed trailer.

Based on the driver's relevant training and experience, he had little, if any, reason to believe the accident trailer and the hump crossing were incompatible. Consequently, he would have had no concern about traversing it, even if he had been fully rested. Therefore, while it appears likely that the driver was fatigued from lack of sleep, his actions in attempting to traverse the crossing were entirely consistent with his experience.

Driver's Actions After Becoming Lodged -- The fact that the driver did not notify anyone in authority after his vehicle became lodged was also a function of his training, his experience, and the circumstances rather than an indication of fatigue. After he became stuck, his focus was entirely on removing the truck rather than stopping a train. Since he had no training on what to do once he was stuck, and since no emergency notification information was posted near the crossing advising him to contact the railroad, he acted in accordance with his experience by asking his brother to try to pull him off the crossing with a pickup truck. In postaccident interviews, the driver said it had not occurred to him that he should call the police or any other authority to notify them of his situation. Even if it had occurred to him to call someone, he would not have tried to call the railroad to stop the train, because he was not aware that this could be done.

It is clear that the driver's experience provided him with only one way to address the problem, which was to move the truck. In fact, everything the driver did from the time he realized that he could not complete his assigned work at Lexington until his truck was struck by the train was totally consistent with his training and experience. The Safety Board therefore concludes that although the driver may have been fatigued at the time his truck became lodged on the crossing, fatigue did not influence the decisions he made or the actions he took before or after his truck became lodged on the crossing.

This driver's actions after becoming lodged were not unique, but rather were typical of what other drivers have done in similar accidents. Of the 16 lowbed vehicle/train collisions investigated by the Safety Board, 12 cases involved no attempt by the drivers to contact appropriate authorities before the collision occurred. In six cases, trucks were lodged, on average, about 15 minutes before the collisions occurred. The Safety Board thus concludes that, like many truckdrivers, this driver was untrained in grade crossing safety and emergency notification procedures and was therefore unprepared to react appropriately to this situation.

In a meeting held in October 1995 concerning this accident, industry representatives stated that after becoming lodged on a crossing, a driver should notify authorities of the potential hazard and proceed to dislodge the vehicle. This position is reiterated in the American Trucking Associations' manual, which states that drivers operating lowbed trailers should avoid places—like—hump crossings—where there are significant changes in road grade. The manual further advises that if a driver becomes lodged on a crossing, he should call authorities, give the crossing location, and notify the railroad.

The Safety Board believes that the truckdriver should have contacted the local police immediately after becoming lodged. Although it appears he did not have a working telephone available in the tractor, he could have walked to either his brother's or his cousin's house nearby and used the telephone there. If he had contacted the local police or dialed 911, the railroad could have been notified.

Because time is critical when a vehicle becomes lodged on a grade crossing, it is imperative that a railroad be notified as soon as possible to allow them the greatest opportunity to notify any trains en route to the blocked crossing. In this accident, 30 to 35 minutes elapsed between the time the vehicle became lodged and the train reached the crossing. The Safety Board reconstructed the time that it likely would have taken for a call to 911 to have reached CSXT, and for a CSXT dispatcher to reach the train crew. The reconstruction suggested the process would take no more than 4 minutes. That would have been sufficient time for the train to have stopped short of the accident crossing. Consequently, the Safety Board concludes that had the driver taken the appropriate action and notified authorities shortly after becoming lodged, this accident would probably not have occurred.

It is possible that, had emergency notification information been posted prominently at the crossing, the driver would have seen it and would have reacted differently. If the driver had seen such information, he would have known immediately that he should notify someone of the hazard after he became lodged, and he would have known whom to notify. Thus, the Safety Board concludes that, had emergency notification information been posted at the accident crossing, the truckdriver may have used it to notify the railroad, thereby avoiding the accident.

Motor Carrier Involvement

As shown by this accident, the motor carrier did not properly manage its driver's activities on job assignments performed after normal business hours. The carrier dispatched the driver on a job without knowing exactly what the job entailed or how long it would take the driver to complete the job, which made it difficult to ensure conformance with applicable hours-of-service regulations. Compounding the problem, it was difficult for the driver to reach the carrier after normal business hours: No one was available in the carrier's office, and the driver's cellular phone provided only limited service in remote areas.

Further, the carrier had no contingency plan in place to deal with driver emergencies; in fact, the motor carrier was not aware of this accident until 4 hours after it occurred. The carrier had not provided any formal or informal training to the accident driver regarding what to do in emergency situations. The Safety Board thus concludes that the carrier did not properly manage the driver's job assignments after normal business hours or provide any training for emergency situations.

Grade Crossing Safety

Although this accident raised important issues involving passenger train safety, similar accidents involving freight trains also represent a significant threat to public safety. For that reason, this analysis will address countermeasures in grade crossing safety that apply to railroads in all modes of service.

Hump Crossings -- The Safety Board looked at several potential countermeasures that would improve driver awareness of hump crossings and possibly reduce the likelihood of collisions between trains and lowbed trucks. The only countermeasures that would be totally effective in preventing hump crossing accidents in the future would be to permanently close, correct, or eliminate (through such means as overpasses or tunnels) all hump crossings. Unfortunately, such countermeasures are not always feasible, meaning that other, more realistic or more readily achievable measures for reducing hump crossing accidents must be considered, such as:

- Installing appropriate signs at hump crossings to warn lowbed vehicle operators of potential hazards;

- Educating lowbed vehicle operators and other motorists on the dangers of traveling over hump crossings, and advising them of what to do when vehicles become lodged/stalled; and

- Implementing emergency notification systems.

Currently, no national data base identifies hump crossings. A review of the DOT/AAR inventory on grade crossings revealed that it does not include vertical profile information, nor is this information documented in any other existing data base. The Safety Board believes that the DOT/AAR inventory can be expanded in a cost-effective manner to include vertical profile data. The survey teams that currently collect state grade crossing data for inclusion into the DOT/AAR inventory could easily be trained to make vertical profile measurements and record this information. This would allow the identification of existing crossings that do not meet the AASHTO standards for highway vertical profiles. Thus, the Safety Board believes that the DOT/AAR inventory should be upgraded to include vertical profile data, which would permit States and local agencies to readily identify potentially hazardous crossings.

If a grade crossing has a high vertical profile and there are no immediate plans to close or correct the crossing, then advisory warning signs are warranted as an interim measure until a permanent solution is available. The purpose of any advisory warning sign, according to Part II-C of the MUTCD, is to "warn traffic of existing or potentially hazardous conditions on or adjacent to a highway or street. Warning signs require caution on the part of the vehicle operator and may call for reduction of speed or a maneuver in the interest of his own safety and that of other vehicle operators and pedestrians."

On June 12, 1995, 9 years after the Safety Board issued Safety Recommendation R-86-50 asking the FHWA to require that warning signs be installed at hump crossings, the FHWA published a notice of proposed amendments to the MUTCD requesting comments on a proposed warning sign for substandard vertical curves over railroad crossings. In light of the fact that so much time has already elapsed since this issue was first presented to the FHWA, and since the need for effective warnings at hump crossings has not diminished, the Safety Board believes that the proposed changes to the MUTCD to include warning signs for hump crossings should be implemented without further delay.

Recent interviews and previous accident investigations conducted by the Safety Board have revealed that the degree of communication and cooperation between railroads and public entities regarding grade crossing activities varies widely. Railroad and public officials tend to communicate more on activities that involve funding of active crossings or the installation and maintenance of active warning devices, or that are likely to generate public complaints. The same level of communication does not exist when it comes to other crossing maintenance activities, particularly as they relate to passive crossings. CSXT, which operates more than 20,000 miles of track, performs crossing profile maintenance to ensure track vertical and horizontal alignment and adequate drainage, while State, local, and sometimes private entities are responsible for maintaining the alignment of the crossing approaches. When crossing maintenance is performed, CSXT does not always advise respective entities of these activities. By the same token, in some cases local entities perform work to realign crossing approaches without informing the railroads. Thus, the Safety Board concludes that railroads and public entities do not routinely communicate with each other on grade crossing maintenance activities.

This is an important issue, since the Safety Board believes that when tracks and/or roadway approaches are realigned, adjacent roadway approaches and/or tracks also should be realigned (raised) commensurately; otherwise, a hump crossing is created. The Safety Board believes that railroads and public entities should work more closely with each other on crossing maintenance activities to prevent the creation of hump crossings. When problem crossings are identified, railroad and highway entities should coordinate efforts to close or take appropriate corrective action to eliminate those crossings. Until that can be achieved, those entities should post warning signs and provide emergency information at all hump crossings. Further, they should consider using other alternatives, such as education programs, to enhance hump crossing awareness among commercial vehicle drivers and other motorists.

Emergency Notification -- In 1986, the Safety Board issued Safety Recommendations R-86-48 and -55 asking that the FRA and the FHWA work together to develop and require a system in each state similar to the State of Texas' toll-free emergency notification system. After 5 years the Safety Board classified these recommendations "Closed--Acceptable Alternate Action," recognizing that some promotional activities had been undertaken by the two Federal agencies. Unfortunately, the implementation of emergency notification systems has been slow; in the past 9 years, only two other States (Delaware and Connecticut) have introduced grade crossing emergency notification systems. The Safety Board notes that several railroads have recognized the value of the toll-free emergency notification systems and have developed their own systems for use either by the public or by law enforcement or other public officials.

The most striking aspect of all the public systems is the fact that the general public has welcomed them and has readily used the systems to report problems at grade crossings. Thus, the Safety Board believes that existing emergency notifications systems have proven their value and should be implemented nationwide. Each new system should, at a minimum, contain the following:

- A toll-free telephone number directed to a communications center that is staffed at all hours during which trains are operated;

- Permanently posted signage located at each grade crossing providing information on the railroad, the toll-free telephone number, the crossing DOT/AAR inventory number, and the name of the road or street on which the crossing is located; and

- A program to inform appropriate law enforcement and emergency response agencies of the availability of the system and to advise them on its use.

Most existing systems service active crossings, the theory being that (1) active crossings are more heavily traveled and (2) the primary purpose of the public notification system is to allow the timely reporting of malfunctioning signals. The fact is, however, that a blocked crossing represents a hazard fully equal to that of a malfunctioning signal. Further, crossing blockages or similar problems are as likely to occur at passive as at active crossings, and they represent a similar potential risk in terms of injuries and property damage. The Safety Board therefore believes that emergency notification systems should service passive, as well as active, crossings.

To make countermeasures effective in the shortest possible time, the Safety Board believes that emergency notification systems should be developed and implemented by all Class I railroads[26] and railroad systems on all their crossings. The Safety Board also recognizes that similar systems may be appropriate for some of the smaller railroads and transit systems and believes that associations representing these entities, such as the American Short Line Railroad Association and the American Public Transit Association, respectively, should encourage their memberships to develop and implement similar notification systems.

Further, the Operation Lifesaver program should work with the Class I railroads and railroads systems and with the smaller railroad and transit systems to increase public awareness (including awareness among trucking groups) of these systems, and to advise law enforcement and the applicable emergency response communities of relevant emergency telephone numbers.

Commercial Truckdriver Training, Education, and Testing -- Several industry training manuals and advisory programs address hump crossings. Specifically, the ATA and the TTMA in their training manual and technical bulletins have published information that provides some guidance on hump crossings. In response to Safety Board recommendations, the FHWA, in 1986 and again in 1989, published and disseminated "On Guard" bulletins to alert truckdrivers to the problem of

---

[26]A railroad with an annual gross operating revenue in excess of $50 million based on 1978 dollars.

high-profile grade crossings. Although this material may be widely distributed amongst larger motor carriers who actively participate in the national industry groups, it is unlikely that the information receives wide distribution among the smaller, local carriers like O&J that are engaged in interstate and intrastate operations but are not members of these groups. Thus, many truckdrivers employed in smaller operations may not be aware of the consequences of driving low-ground-clearance vehicles over hump crossings.

There are at least 168,000 public and 108,000 private grade crossings nationwide. Large commercial vehicles use these crossings frequently in the conduct of business. Clearly, all truckdrivers should be educated on the hazards of grade crossings in general and hump crossings in particular. They need to be advised on how to avoid these crossings, and on how to notify police and/or railroad officials when emergencies occur. One approach to doing this, which will reach all new drivers, is through the CDL program. All commercial operators of large trucks (over 26,000 pounds gross vehicle weight) must obtain a State-issued CDL by taking an examination that tests their knowledge and skills in motor carrier operation and safety. The CDL manual does contain some information on hump crossings; however, current CDL tests administered by the States do not ask questions about grade crossing safety.

The Safety Board believes that the CDL manual should be expanded to include more specific information on the operation of lowbed vehicles over hump crossings, including avoidance techniques, and should provide information on making emergency notifications to police and railroad officials when commercial vehicles become stalled or lodged on crossings. Further, the Safety Board believes that CDL tests administered by the States should include questions that test truckdrivers on their general knowledge of grade crossing safety, their awareness of the hazards of hump crossings, and their knowledge of related emergency notification procedures.

The Operation Lifesaver program has been successful in educating the general public about grade crossing safety. Recently OL officials have directed significant attention to trucking groups. Representatives of OL stated that they will include awareness of hump crossings in their truck program. The Safety Board commends the efforts of OL, and believes that it should not only expand its educational program to include hump-crossing awareness, but should also target the expanded program to groups that are not exposed to industry programs. The Safety Board further believes that OL should expand the North and South Carolina initiative that provides emergency personnel with railroad industry telephone numbers to use when vehicles become lodged or stalled on crossings.

The Safety Board further believes that the ATA can play a significant role in enhancing grade crossing safety for all drivers by highlighting the hazards presented by hump crossings in ATA in-service training programs. This in-service training should also address emergency notification procedures to be used in the event of a grade crossing emergency. Drivers who become lodged at a grade crossing should be instructed to look first for any posted emergency notification information. If such information is not available, those drivers should be advised to dial 911 or contact the local police and ask that the railroad be notified.

Emergency Response

The Allendale County deputy sheriff was the first official to arrive on the scene. He interviewed the truckdriver, made minimal observations of the train, and advised the dispatcher that emergency medical assistance was not needed. Later, a South Carolina Highway Patrol trooper arrived on the scene and, seeing bedding sheets lying in the ballast, called to request medical assistance. Approximately 42 minutes elapsed between the 911 call reporting the accident and the first request for medical help. If any of the train occupants had sustained serious injuries, their outcomes may have been adversely affected by this delay.

When grade crossing accidents occur, particularly involving derailed passenger trains, responding law enforcement officers should immediately make detailed observations and inquires about possible injured passengers. This is standard procedure among law enforcement agencies, and while the Safety Board has found that it is followed in most cases, in this accident, it was not. If the initial responding police officer had made a proper assessment of the seriousness of the accident and the potential for injuries, he would have determined immediately that medical help was needed. Thus, the Safety Board concludes that the initial responding police officer made no effort to assess possible injuries among train passengers and crew before informing the dispatcher that medical assistance was not needed.

The Allendale County Sheriff's Department had a longstanding policy requiring deputies to immediately request that the appropriate emergency response units be dispatched when incidents such as train derailments occur. Although this policy was not adhered to in this accident, the Allendale County Sheriff's Department has assured Safety Board investigators that this policy will be followed for future incidents involving potential mass casualties.

After being notified, the Allendale Fire Department and County Emergency Services responded appropriately, quickly administered medical treatment to injured persons, and evacuated the train occupants in a timely manner.

CONCLUSIONS

1. The truckdriver and the traincrew were qualified and were not suffering from any contributory medical problems, and there is no evidence to suggest that they were under the influence of alcohol or other drugs at the time of the accident.

2. The condition of the track, the operation of the signals, the mechanical condition of the train and truck, and the weather were not factors in this accident.

3. The initial responding police officer made no effort to assess possible injuries among train passengers and crew before informing the dispatcher that medical assistance was not needed.

4. The Allendale Fire Department and County Emergency Services responded appropriately, quickly administered medical treatment to injured persons, and efficiently evacuated the train.

5. Even if the train operating crew had seen the truck on the crossing at their first opportunity, they would not have had sufficient distance to stop the train and avoid the collision.

6. The truck, as configured, could not safely travel over the crossing because of the crossing's substandard geometric characteristics.

7. Although the driver may have been fatigued at the time his truck became lodged on the crossing, fatigue did not influence the decisions he made or the actions he took before or after his truck became lodged on the crossing.

8. Like many truckdrivers, this driver was untrained in grade crossing safety and emergency notification procedures and was therefore unprepared to react appropriately to this situation.

9. Had the driver taken the appropriate action and notified authorities shortly after becoming lodged, this accident would probably not have occurred.

10. Had emergency notification information been posted at the accident crossing, the truckdriver may have used it to notify the railroad, thereby avoiding the accident.

11. The carrier did not properly manage the driver's job assignments after normal business hours or provide any training for emergency situations.

12. Railroads and public entities do not routinely communicate with each other on grade crossing maintenance activities.

PROBABLE CAUSE

The Safety Board determines that the probable cause of this accident was the motor carrier's failure to provide to the driver appropriate guidance to respond to emergency situations. This led to the truckdriver's failure both to understand that the substandard profile of the Boogaloo Road grade crossing was incompatible with the truck he was operating, and to notify the appropriate railroad and emergency personnel of the blocked crossing. Contributing to the accident was the absence of emergency notification information that the driver may have used to notify the railroad of the blocked crossing.

RECOMMENDATIONS

As a result of its investigation of this accident, the National Transportation Safety Board makes the following recommendations:

--to the Secretary of Transportation:

> Amend the Department of Transportation/Association of American Railroads Grade Crossing Inventory data base to include vertical profile information on all highway/rail grade crossings in the United States. (Class II, Priority Action) (H-96-1)

> Encourage and coordinate efforts between the railroad industry and State and local highway transportation officials to identify substandard grade crossing profiles (hump crossings) and close or take appropriate corrective action to eliminate them. (Class II, Priority Action) (H-96-2)

> Encourage States to post warning notices at hump crossings where high profiles present potential hazards for highway vehicles and where such hazardous profiles cannot be corrected in a timely manner. (Class II, Priority Action) (H-96-3)

> Develop procedures and processes that will facilitate improved communication and coordination between the railroad industry and State and local highway transportation officials regarding crossing maintenance activities so as to prevent the creation of hump crossings. (Class II, Priority Action) (H-96-4)

--to the Federal Highway Administration:

> Adopt the proposed changes that are published in the notice of proposed amendments to the *Manual on Uniform Traffic Control Devices* regarding warning signs for substandard vertical profiles at railroad grade crossings. (Class II, Priority Action) (H-96-5)

--to the American Public Transit Association:

> Encourage your members to develop and implement, without delay, a 24-hour toll-free emergency notification telephone system for use by the public in promptly reporting emergencies at all your members' highway/rail grade crossings, both active and passive, and provide information at each

crossing to inform the public of the 24-hour telephone system. (Class II, Priority Action) (R-96-1)

--to the American Association of Motor Vehicle Administrators:

Revise the commercial driver's license manual to include specific information on hump crossings, and ensure that truckdrivers are tested on their knowledge of grade crossing safety, with special emphasis on hump crossings. (Class II, Priority Action) (H-96-6)

Revise the commercial driver's license manual to include information on grade crossing emergency notification procedures, and ensure that truckdrivers are tested on their knowledge of these procedures. (Class II, Priority Action) (H-96-7)

--to the American Trucking Associations, Inc.:

Advise your membership of the circumstances of this accident, and during in-service training for all drivers, highlight the potential hazards associated with moving lowbed trailers over hump grade crossings. Include specific instructions for notifying authorities when emergencies or hazardous conditions exist at grade crossings. (Class II, Priority Action) (H-96-8)

--to the American Short Line Railroad Association:

Encourage your members to develop and implement, without delay, a 24-hour toll-free emergency notification telephone system for use by the public in promptly reporting emergencies at all your members' highway/rail grade crossings, both active and passive, and provide information at each crossing to inform the public of the 24-hour telephone system. (Class II, Priority Action) (R-96-2)

--to Operation Lifesaver, Inc.

In conjunction with appropriate trucking industry groups, expand your existing programs to educate truckdrivers who are not exposed to industry programs on the hazards of hump grade crossings. (Class II, Priority Action) (H-96-9)

In cooperation with the Class I railroads, railroad systems, the American Short Line Railroad Association, and the American Public Transit Association, expand your existing programs to inform the general public and law enforcement and emergency response agencies of grade crossing emergency notification programs within their respective States. (Class II, Priority Action) (H-96-10)

--to Class I railroads and railroad systems:

> Develop and implement, without delay, a 24-hour toll-free emergency notification telephone system for use by the public in promptly reporting emergencies at all your highway/rail grade crossings, both active and passive, and provide information at each crossing to inform the public of the 24-hour telephone system. (Class II, Priority Action) (R-96-3)

--to O&J Gordon Trucking Company:

> Establish a program than ensures driver conformance with hours-of-service and medical certification requirements. (Class II, Priority Action) (H-96-11)

> Establish a contingency plan that addresses on-the-road emergencies and that provides drivers with guidance in dealing with potentially hazardous situations such as having a vehicle stall or become lodged on a grade crossing. (Class II, Priority Action) (H-96-12)

BY THE NATIONAL TRANSPORTATION SAFETY BOARD

JAMES E. HALL
Chairman

ROBERT T. FRANCIS II
Vice Chairman

JOHN A. HAMMERSCHMIDT
Member

JOHN J. GOGLIA
Member

GEORGE W. BLACK, Jr.
Member

March 11, 1996

APPENDIX A

Investigation

The National Transportation Safety Board was notified of this accident at 4:20 a.m. on May 2, 1995. Accident investigators dispatched from the Safety Board's Atlanta, Georgia, regional office arrived at 10:00 a.m. on May 2, and investigators from the Safety Board's headquarters in Washington, D.C., arrived on scene at 11:00 a.m. A 13-person team conducted the on-scene investigation, concluding the on-scene work on May 4, 1995.

Participating in the investigation were representatives of O&J Gordon Trucking; CSX Transportation, Inc.; the National Railroad Passenger Corporation (Amtrak); the Allendale County sheriffs department, fire department, rescue service, and police department; the Federal Railroad Administration; and the Federal Highway Administration.

Hearing/Deposition

The Safety Board did not hold a public hearing or deposition proceedings in conjunction with this investigation. On May 2, 1995, the Safety Board obtained sworn testimony from the engineer, the assistant engineer, the conductor, and the assistant conductor.

APPENDIX B

Injury Information

Injuries in this accident have been coded to the revised 1990 Abbreviated Injury Scale of the American Association for Automotive Medicine, which is a standard system of assessing injury severity.

Abbreviated injury scale

Injuries	Truckdriver	Traincrew	Train Passengers	Total
AIS-1 Minor	0	4	29	33
AIS-2 Moderate	0	0	0	0
AIS-3 Serious	0	0	0	0
AIS-4 Severe	0	0	0	0
AIS-5 Critical	0	0	0	0
AIS-6 Unsurvivable	0	0	0	0
AIS-0 None	1	5	250	256
AIS-9 Unknown	0	0	0	0
Total	1	9	279	289

APPENDIX C

Existing Grade Crossing Emergency Notification Systems

Texas

In 1983, the State of Texas, with the support of the major railroads operating within the state, enacted the "Railroad Grade Crossing Information Act" (the Act). The Act directed the Texas Department of Public Safety (DPS) to establish a toll-free telephone service for the reception of calls reporting malfunctions at highway/railroad grade crossings.

The State Department of Highways and Public Transportation (SDHPT)[1] was required to attach a sign displaying the toll-free telephone number and the DOT/AAR inventory number to each train-activated grade crossing active warning device on the State-maintained highway and road system. This Act was later amended to include train-activated grade crossings on county roads as well. One unique outcome in the implementation of the Act was that SDHPT employees were allowed by the railroads to enter their private property and post the information signs.

The Act contained a series of legal protections as described below:

A court may not hold the State, an agency or subdivision of the State, or a railroad company liable for damages caused by an action taken under this Act or failure to perform a duty imposed by this Act.

No evidence may be introduced in a trial or judicial proceeding that such service exists or is relied upon by the State or railroad company.

A State agency is not required to make or retain permanent records or information obtained in implementation of this Act.

The Texas 1-800 system is basically a clearinghouse for telephone messages relating to problems at grade crossings. DPS emergency operators staff this system 24-hours a day. Any information received by the DPS operators through this system is forwarded to the appropriate railroad within a matter of minutes. DPS operators indicated that they receive three or four calls on blocked crossings daily. The majority of the blockages are rail cars blocking the grade crossing; however, they have received calls where motor vehicles were blocking grade crossings. Signal malfunctions represent most of the reported calls to the system.

In 1989, the Federal Railroad Administration (FRA) completed an evaluation of the Texas 1-800 system. A review of crossing problems highlighted in 47 months of calls reported indicated the following:

---

[1]The Texas Department of Highways and Public Transportation (SDHPT) is now known as the Texas Department of Transportation (TXDOT).

Crossing Problem	Number of Reports	Percent of Total
Warning devices	8446	92.7
Signs and markings	13	0.1
Crossings blocked/other highway problem near crossing	125	1.4
Track and structure	321	3.5
Trespassers	7	0.1
Sight distance	12	0.1
Train operations	29	0.3
Other	166	1.8
Total	9119	100.0

About 4,600 active grade crossing locations in Texas are signed; approximately 14,000 grade crossings are not signed. The Texas Department of Transportation (TXDOT) reported that the signs are made in the Texas penal institutions at a cost of $22 per sign. Two signs are placed at each grade crossing location, and installation takes approximately 1/2 half hour. The civil engineer responsible for this program at TXDOT indicated that vandalism of the signs is rare.

The TXDOT also includes information on the 1-800 system in their newly issued application and permit form for oversized and overweight vehicles. The Texas permit regulations issued September 1995 explain the use of the railroad grade crossing emergency hotline, including the requirement for commercial vehicle operators to immediately call the 1-800 number if their vehicle is lodged on railroad tracks.

Delaware

In 1988, the State of Delaware Department of Transportation (DELDOT) and Consolidated Rail Corporation (Conrail) initiated an agreement that the railroad would maintain a toll-free telephone emergency notification system available to the public with signs at Conrail's public grade crossings. The stated purpose of this system was to provide the public as well as local agencies a means to immediately report a crossing problem that could otherwise go unreported for an excessive period. The 1-800 emergency number dials directly to Conrail's communications and signal trouble desk in Columbus, Ohio. Should the problem be a malfunctioning signal, the trouble desk dispatches a signal maintainer to the location and logs the call and the response time. Originally, the agreement was tied to funds provided by the DELDOT if Conrail maintained and repaired malfunctioning grade crossing signals within a specified time. The agreement terminated in 1993 due to funding limitations. The State paid $1 million to Conrail during the 5-year period. Currently, Conrail is providing funding to maintain the 1-800 toll-free system in operation.

Of Delaware's 451 public grade crossings, 183 (41 percent) have emergency notification signs installed. Two of the involved agencies (DELDOT and the Delaware Transit Corporation) reported they would like to reactivate the program and expand the 1-800 system to the other five railroads operating within Delaware. The previous Delaware Railroad Administrator, in a memorandum to the DELDOT Transportation Trust Fund Administrator dated June 16, 1994, stated the benefits with continuing the maintenance agreement with Conrail would include

more efficient reporting of defects;
reduced malfunctioning time of signals;
increased confidence in warning signals;
reduced liability;
improved relations with the public;
an improved DELDOT and railroad(s) working relationship.

The Delaware Railroad Administration (and its successor, the Delaware Transit Corporation) endorsed the continuation and expansion of the funding for the 1-800 program.

The 1-800 system concept is supported by Conrail. Although the State of Delaware has not funded the program since 1993, Conrail continues with the program because the railroad does not want the public to lose confidence in the signal systems at grade crossings. Although no records have been kept on accidents prevented by this system, Conrail has some records indicating, in broad categories, the types of calls received. For example, in 1993, 326 calls were made to Conrail's trouble desk. Of these, 170 (52 percent) were the result of a signal component failure. For 84 calls (26 percent), Conrail arrived at the location and there was no cause found for the report. Another 72 calls (22 percent) were the result of reported vandalism, weather, or accidents.

DELDOT makes the crossing signs at a cost of $22.40 per sign. Two signs are installed at each of Conrail's active-warning-device grade crossings in Delaware. Conrail's engineer responsible for this program indicated that reported damage to the signs on location was minimal. This also was confirmed by officials in the Delaware Transit Corporation and DELDOT.

Connecticut

In 1990, Connecticut enacted Public Act 90-329 requiring railroad companies to erect signs with the 911 emergency telecommunications number at all grade crossings with gates or signals. The Act specified that the provision did not apply to any railroad company operating trains that do not exceed 25 miles per hour. The purpose of the sign is to advise the public to call 911 upon the malfunctioning of any grade crossing gates or signals. Connecticut Department of Transportation (CTDOT) requires each railroad company to maintain logs, subject to the inspection of the Department, listing all reports of the malfunctioning of grade crossing gates and signals. The 911 operator forwards the telephone reports to local police, who notify the railroad of the reported condition. The railroad company must document all investigations and actions taken by the company to repair malfunctioning gates or signals. Each railroad company must report to the local municipality all actions taken as a result of these calls.

Currently, about 150 (28 percent) of the 530 grade crossings in Connecticut have signs installed. The CTDOT estimates that the cost of the signs and the bracket are about $15 each. There are two signs at each grade crossing location. The railroad is responsible for installing the signs.

Although there has been no evaluation of the 911 emergency telecommunication system for grade crossings, CTDOT indicates that an evaluation is planned in the near future.

Canada

Canadian National's (CN) Signal and Communications Department of the Southern Ontario District (SOD) developed and implemented a 1-800 24-hour emergency notification system in July 1994. This effort was also supported by SOD's Safety and Loss Control Department and CN police, who established the communication center. The stated objectives of the 1-800 system are to document safety issues at grade crossings, enhance the safety level of the railroad, and foster a closer relationship with the general public and employees.

There are about 2,000 grade crossings in the SOD; all public active warning device-installed crossings and passive crossings are signed with the emergency number and crossing location. The oldest of the signs have been in place for 2 years, and CN staff indicated that these signs are still serviceable. They are visible and have not been tampered with or destroyed by vandals. The SOD signs are computer generated, cost about $5 each, and are installed by a signal maintainer . At active-warning-device locations, the sign is placed on the bungalow (the case that holds the electrical panel for the crossing). At passive crossings, the emergency signs are placed on the back of the crossbuck. SOD's district engineer estimated that the total cost to sign his entire District at all crossings was about $20,000.

CN Police are responsible for incoming calls. The police dispatchers directly contact the Ontario Provincial Police or CN's chief dispatcher if a call is received with life-threatening possibilities. Trains are halted, if such action is warranted. Malfunctioning signal calls result in the signals being checked by CN's signal maintainers. CN Police have not yet assessed the number and type of calls received, but an evaluation is planned in the future. The majority of calls the police believe are malfunctioning signal reports or blocked crossings. CN reports that the railroad does not have hump crossing problems similar to those in the U.S.

On August 1, 1995, CN's Southern Ontario District and Northern Ontario District merged to become the Great Lakes District. The Great Lakes district engineer reported that an additional 500 grade crossings of about 1,000 in the old Northern Ontario District have the emergency information posted. He also noted that the Maritime and Laurentian Districts have merged into the Champlain District, and he said he fully expects that this new district will move toward application of the 1-800 emergency system soon.

The Norfolk Southern Corporation (NS)

In December 1994, NS developed and implemented its 1-800 Crossing Hot Line. The communication center for the Crossing Hot line incoming calls is manned by the NS Police.

NS has approximately 27,000 grade crossings of which 17,000 (63 percent) are public grade crossings, and 10,000 (37 percent) are private grade crossings. Of the 27,000 grade crossings, 7,000 (26 percent) have active warning devices. NS officials stated that all active warning device locations have two installed retro-reflective decals: One is placed 5 feet above ground level on the flashing light crossing signal mast, and the other is placed approximately 5 feet out from the mast on the white section of the grade crossing gate arm. The decals are quite visible, and the NS manager of grade crossing safety reported that the decals have not been tampered or destroyed by vandals. The cost of the NS' signing program for all active warning device locations has been $16,395. Because signs primarily are used to report signal malfunctions, NS has not signed passive grade crossing locations. The decals are installed by signal maintainers as adjunct duties.

NS Police are responsible for incoming calls on this 1-800 system. The police dispatchers directly contact division chief dispatchers. The NS Police do not try to screen the calls; this is the responsibility of each division chief dispatcher's office. The dispatcher notifies local crossing and signal maintainers and logs all telephone messages into a computer system. The 1-800 Crossing Hotline during the period January through July 1995 received 1,061 calls. NS reports that its dispatch offices have reported this system has already been successful in many instances in safely stopping trains. The NS manager of grade crossing safety has requested information from NS personnel on the possible application of the 1-800 Crossing Hotline decal at passive crossing locations.

Santa Fe Railway

Since 1991, the Santa Fe Railway has had a 1-800 toll-free emergency telephone notification system. Currently, about 3,000 grade crossings across the Santa Fe system have had a stencil applied to the grade crossing's cabinet (bungalow). The out-of-pocket cost for this system was $20,000, or about $6.67 per grade crossing location. The labor cost for applying the stencil to the bungalow is not included in this reported expense, primarily because the installation is done as adjunct duty. Information provided by this stenciled application includes the railroad's name, the street address, the milepost location, the DOT/AAR Inventory number, and the 1-800 toll-free telephone number. The stenciled lettering is large enough for engineers on passing trains to provide reports of unusual problems at grade crossings.

Calls made to the 1-800 emergency telephone number go directly to Santa Fe's police communications center. The calls are screened by police dispatchers. The railroad reports that it does not keep separate logs on the types of calls it receives, and no evaluation of the system has been made. If a call reports a serious condition, such as a motor vehicle blocking a grade crossing, police dispatch immediately reports such information to the railroad's chief dispatcher so that any train near that grade crossing will be notified. Santa Fe reported that they have averted some blocked crossing accidents because of timely reports through the 1-800 toll-free emergency telephone system.

CSX Transportation, Inc. (CSXT)

On July 12, 1995, Safety Board staff met with officials of CSXT, who informed Safety Board staff that they are establishing a 1-800 toll-free emergency telephone system for public use. The system became operational in February 1996. Also, CSXT representatives indicated that they intend to install appropriate signage at all crossing locations on their system.

Other U.S. Railroads

Two domestic railroads have 1-800 emergency toll-free telephone numbers that are not posted at grade crossing locations. The Burlington Northern Railroad Company (BN) has a 1-800 number; however, the number is only provided to law enforcement officers and public officials for use in emergencies. A serious grade crossing accident could be reported by local officials on the BN number. The Union Pacific Railroad Company (UP) also has a 1-800 toll-free emergency telephone system, but the number is not posted at grade crossing locations. Since 1992, the UP has distributed about 15,000 cards announcing the number to local law enforcement and public officials. Calls to this system are forwarded directly to a trouble desk at UP's central dispatch location, Harriman Center. This desk is staffed 24-hours a day by a trained signal technician who screens the calls. This system is called the "Grade Crossing Emergency Hot-Line."

Foreign Railroads

The Safety Board reviewed the French National Railway (SNCF) emergency notification system. Emergency telephone call boxes are used on the SNCF system. The SNCF reported that 9,400 (83 percent) of the country's 11,300 active-device grade crossing locations are equipped with the call boxes. There are a total of 21,200 grade crossings on the SNCF system.

The SNCF keeps no log of the calls received by this system; however, the railroad reported that there have been emergency train stops made after calls were received through the system. The SNCF indicates that there have been some limited cases of vandalism of the call boxes.

The Safety Board also reviewed the Japanese system for emergency notifications. Many of Japan's grade crossings include an emergency button intended for use by motorists in the event a vehicle stalls or is otherwise disabled on a crossing. The button activates the wayside signal system that alerts the train operator of a problem at the grade crossing.

Operation Lifesaver (OL)

After meetings with the Safety Board, both the North Carolina and South Carolina Operation Lifesaver coordinators developed and distributed a flyer that clearly informed emergency personnel of how and whom to telephone in the event a vehicle becomes lodged on a crossing. A copy of the flyer was sent to every law enforcement agency in each state.

At meetings with the Safety Board on October 10, 1995, and October 21, 1995, Operation Lifesaver officials expressed their intent to expand the successful programs implemented in North and South Carolina, and to develop others to insure that emergency notification of problems at grade crossings becomes a national project.

APPENDIX D

Safety Board Findings, Recommendations, and Responses
Regarding Tractor-Lowbed Semitrailer/Train Collisions

On August 23, 1983, Amtrak Train No. 88 struck a tractor lowbed-semitrailer that had become lodged on a grade crossing on the single-track main line grade crossing of the Seaboard System Railroad in Rowland, North Carolina. On November 30, 1983, Amtrak Train No. 98 struck a tractor lowbed-semitrailer that had become lodged on the Seaboard single-track main line grade crossing in Citra, Florida.

In January 1984, the Florida Department of Transportation convened an internal committee to study the problem of hazardous grade crossing profiles as illustrated by the Rowland and Citra accidents. The formation of the committee followed the Safety Board's investigation of the Citra accident and discussions held by Board investigators with local and State officials.

The committee was mandated to pursue an aggressive program of corrective action. Its proposed actions included:

1. Developing a standard roadway (profile) design for grade crossings;
2. Identifying crossings currently not in compliance with the standard;
3. Encouraging local governments to bring crossings into compliance;
4. Suggesting to the railroads that they develop and implement a procedure for coordinating and cooperating with local and State governments to ensure the integrity of the geometric profiles at grade crossings where maintenance has been performed on the track;
5. Developing and implementing a program to install warning signs at crossings identified as having hazardous surface hump profiles; and
6. Encouraging the Florida Truck Association to inform its membership of the hazards of hump crossings.

On August 29, 1984, as a result of its investigation of the Rowland and Citra accidents, the Safety Board recommended to the American Association of State Highway and Transportation Officials (AASHTO):

H-84-69
Review the State safety program dealing with hazardous grade crossing profile conditions now underway in Florida, and promote the adoption within each State of this program or a comparable program developed by an appropriate AASHTO committee.

On March 20, 1989, AASHTO responded to Safety Recommendation H-84-69, advising that when initially considering the recommendation, AASHTO was aware that the Federal Highway Administration (FHWA) at that time had a project underway to revise the 1978

Railroad-Highway Grade Crossing Handbook. The revision, completed in November 1986, included a section on vertical alignment that outlines problem areas and several alternative approaches in use by the States, including the Florida program, to deal with those problems. Safety Recommendation H-84-69 was placed in a "Closed--Acceptable Alternate Action" status on July 14, 1989.

The Safety Board also found that there was a need to consider vehicle ground clearance when designing and maintaining roadway profiles, and that there was a need for coordination between railroads and highway departments concerning railroad/highway grade crossing maintenance. On August 29, 1984, the Safety Board issued two recommendations to the Association of American Railroads (AAR):

R-84-35
Establish the specifications stated in Section 1.2, "Profile and Alignment of Crossings and Approaches," of the "Manual for Railway Engineering" of the American Railway Engineering Association as the minimum acceptable specifications for railroad\highway grade crossings.

R-84-36
Encourage all member railroads to coordinate activity related to track maintenance with local and State governments to preserve the integrity of the profiles at railroad/highway grade crossings.

Regarding Safety Recommendation R-84-35, on September 19, 1984, the AAR responded:

. . . [W]e agree with the substance or thrust of your recommendation, but must point out that it should have been directed to the appropriate state or federal government highway agencies. . . . [S]tate highway agencies and the Federal Highway Administration should develop such grade crossing profile designs and adopt them, for instance, as AASHTO standards.

The AAR also stated that it believed the FHWA should mandate, by regulation, a minimum road clearance in the design and manufacture of all highway vehicles, and that government highway agencies at all levels must ensure that all new and reconstructed grade crossings reflect a profile that would accommodate vehicles having this minimum road clearance. It went on to say that government highway agencies should also identify all crossings that do not meet the standard profile design, erect and maintain appropriate advance warning signs on crossings having a non-standard profile, and prohibit access thereto by low clearance vehicles.

On January 10, 1985, the Safety Board responded that it believed the railroads' active participation was necessary to effect improvements in hazardous grade crossing profiles and urged the AAR to reconsider the intent of Safety Recommendation R-84-35. The Safety Board placed that recommendation in an "Open--Unacceptable Action" status.

On February 14, 1985, the AAR responded:

> The construction and major reconstruction of public highway-railroad grade crossings is today conducted almost exclusively under the authority, direction, and funding of government highway agencies. The (AAR) would never prescribe or dictate design criteria for highway projects implemented under a public highway program, neither would the involved public highway agency permit such interference by the railroad industry. . . . The railroads would certainly be eager to participate and assist appropriate government highway agencies in the development of any such grade crossing profile designs, but it would be totally inappropriate for the (AAR) or its members to attempt to impose such standards on government agencies.

On June 10, 1985, the Safety Board advised the AAR that the Board believed that AAR's participation in development of grade crossing profile designs with government highway organizations would be welcomed rather than interpreted as interference, and urged the AAR to reconsider its position. After receiving no further response, on June 23, 1987, Safety Recommendation R-84-35 was classified "Closed--Unacceptable Action."

On July 27, 1987, the AAR advised the Safety Board that, although the AAR neither develops or adopts engineering standards and that such responsibility rests with the American Railroad Engineering Association (AREA), the AAR is a strong supporter of grade crossing safety and the then-planned National Conference on Highway-Rail Crossing Safety, pointing out that the conference agenda included a session devoted to the engineering relationship between the roadway and the railroad at or near grade crossings. The AAR requested that the status of Safety Recommendation R-84-35 be reclassified "Closed--Alternate Acceptable Action." The file does not include a Safety Board response to this letter.

Regarding Safety Recommendation R-84-36, on November 5, 1984, the AAR urged the chief operating officers of the member railroads to coordinate track maintenance activity with the appropriate government agencies in order to preserve the integrity of the profile at railroad/highway grade crossings. Safety Recommendation R-84-36 was thus classified "Closed--Acceptable Action" on June 13, 1985.

In its study of 1985 grade crossing accidents[1], the Safety Board concluded that improved advance warning signs could be developed to indicate a variety of hazardous grade crossing situations, particularly limited sight distance, difficult crossing approaches (such as high crossing

---

[1]Safety Study *Passenger/Commuter Train and Motor Vehicle Collisions at Grade Crossings (1985)* (NTSB/SS-86/04).

profiles), and high-speed train operations. As a result of the study, on January 13, 1987, the Safety Board recommended that the FHWA:

R-86-50
Develop and require the use of advance warning signs that clearly inform motor vehicle drivers of particular dangers at grade crossings, including the warning of limited sight distance and high hump profiles.

On May 11, 1987, the FHWA responded to Safety Recommendation R-86-50, advising that changes to the *Manual on Uniform Traffic Control Devices* (MUTCD) were not warranted at that time. The Safety Board responded, advising the FHWA that in view of the number of accidents investigated by the Safety Board in which a limited sight distance or a high-hump-profile surface had been factors, the Board believed that, at a minimum, the MUTCD should indicate specifically that these two warning signs may be warranted at certain locations. Safety Recommendation R-86-50 was classified "Open--Unacceptable Action" on October 2, 1987.

Five accidents involving trucks lodged on hump grade crossings were discussed in the Safety Board's 1988 study of 189 heavy truck accidents[2]. As a result of its investigations, on February 21, 1989, the Safety Board reiterated Safety Recommendation R-86-50, and also recommended that the FHWA:

H-89-22[3]
Identify design criteria to determine what geometric conditions on approaches to grade crossings would create a hazard to low-clearance vehicles and develop geometric design criteria and traffic control systems for mitigating hazards.

On May 27, 1993, the FHWA advised the Safety Board that pages 842-843 of the AASHTO revised railroad grade crossings section of its 1990 edition of AASHTO's *A Policy on Geometric Design of Highways and Streets* included vertical alignment criteria for low-clearance vehicles. On September 16, 1993, the Safety Board classified Safety Recommendation H-89-22 "Closed--Acceptable Action."

Regarding Safety Recommendation R-86-50, on February 22, 1991, the FHWA advised the Safety Board that, although States had been testing the use of warning signs at the approaches to hump crossings, problems regarding when and where such signs should be placed had not been resolved. The FHWA stated:

A vehicle standard is essential for any uniformity (such as the 1/2 inch clearance per foot of axle spacing, 9 inch minimum in the Uniform Vehicle Code), but allowed variations and special permitting are frequent. Reasonable design criteria will not catch the special users most prone to hangup (e.g., lowboys on rural roads, special auto carriers on urban streets), while strict criteria would

---

[2]Safety Study--*Case Summaries of 189 Heavy Truck Accident Investigations* (NTSB/SS-88/05).

[3]This safety recommendation was originally and erroneously numbered H-89-6, and it may be cited by that number in some of the literature relative to this issue.

unnecessarily limit or divert regular vehicles. Adding the uncertainty on where such signs should be placed (last turnaround in rural, every intersecting street in urban?) and the predominance of such crossings on local roads and streets, such a requirement would be premature, if not infeasible. At present the burden must be on the special carriers themselves to identify and only use routes that can accommodate the special or unique vehicles they choose to operate.

The Safety Board responded that it continued to be concerned about and would monitor the issue of high crossing profiles in future grade crossing accidents. Safety Recommendation R-86-50 was classified "Closed--Unacceptable Action" on May 22, 1991.

APPENDIX E

Accident Summaries
Lowbed Vehicle/Train Collisions Investigated by the Safety Board

CASE NO. 1

Safety Board Investigation Number:	N/A
Accident Location:	Church Street, Rowland, North Carolina
Date and Time:	August 25, 1983, 1:10 a.m.
Motor Vehicle Type:	Tractor/lowbed semitrailer
Motor Carrier:	S. L. Balogh Trucking Company Inc.
	Ft. Lauderdale, Florida
Train Involved:	Amtrak, Train No. 88 (Silver Meteor)
Railroad Involved:	Seaboard System Railroad
U.S. DOT/AAR Crossing Number:	N/A
Train-Activated Warning Devices:	Red flashing Lights, gates
Fatalities:	0
Injuries:	29
Estimated Property Damage:	$623,399

Summary:

Northbound Amtrak train No. 88 was operating at an engineer-reported speed of about 65 mph as it approached the Church Street grade crossing in Rowland, North Carolina. The engineer reported that about 1,200 feet from the crossing he saw a semitrailer blocking the crossing, and he applied the train's brakes in emergency. The lead locomotive struck the semitrailer, derailed, overturned on its right side, and slid along the ground. After colliding with and uprighting the lead locomotive, the second locomotive unit and the following mail and baggage dormitory cars were derailed upright.

The collision separated the tractor from the lowbed semitrailer and its cargo, a pavement profile. The gross weight of the highway vehicle and its cargo was 105,820 pounds, and the profile was being transported from Stanhope, New Jersey, to Hialeah Gardens, Florida.

Although the motor carrier had obtained special permits from New Jersey, Pennsylvania, Maryland, Virginia, North Carolina, South Carolina, Georgia, and Florida, the North Carolina permit authorized a maximum gross weight of 103,000 pounds and required that the load be transported only during daylight hours and only on Interstate 95. The motor carrier had instructed the truckdriver to avoid North Carolina scales, and the truck was traveling off its authorized route when it became lodged on the humped grade crossing.

The distance between the semitrailer's kingpin and the first semitrailer axle was 36 feet, 4 inches, and in this configuration the underside of the semitrailer's cargo bed cleared a level roadway by about 7 inches. The 35-foot-wide elevated hump developed a 207.30-foot radius vertical curve profile in the roadway at the crossing.

The 27-year old truckdriver had driven similar equipment for 3 years, mostly transporting heavy equipment in southern Florida. He reported that after becoming lodged on the crossing he attempted to raise the semitrailer frame by operating the hydraulic rams on the semitrailer gooseneck, but was unsuccessful in these attempts in the 5 to- 10 minutes before the collision. He did not attempt to contact the police or the railroad before the collision.

CASE NO. 2

Safety Board Investigation Number:	ATL-84-M-R004
Accident Location:	Citra, Florida, County Road 318
Date and Time:	November 30, 1983, 2:45 p.m.
Motor Vehicle Type:	Tractor/lowbed semitrailer
Motor Carrier:	C & A Earthmovers, Palatka, Florida
Train Involved:	Amtrak, Train No. 98 (Silver Meteor)
Railroad Involved:	Seaboard System Railroad
U.S. DOT/AAR Crossing Number:	625030V
Train-Activated Warning Devices:	Cantilevered red flashing lights, gates, gong.

Fatalities:	0
Injuries:	59
Estimated Property Damage:	$200,119

Summary:

Northbound Amtrak train No. 98 was operating at about 79 mph rounding a curve about 4,000 feet south of the Seaboard System Railroad's main track intersection with Marion County Road 318 in Citra, Florida, when the engineer observed a man on the railroad right-of-way waving his arms and saw a tractor-lowbed semitrailer lodged on the County Road 318 grade crossing. The train's engineer applied the brakes in a service application, and as the train drew closer, he made an emergency application.

The train's speed had been reduced to about 35 mph when it collided with the tractor/semitrailer. The collision separated the tractor from the semitrailer and its cargo, a piece of earth-moving equipment. The collision forced the west rail to tip outward, and the locomotive and the first four cars of the eight-car consist derailed, coming to rest upright, in line, and still coupled.

The earth-moving equipment was being transported under a special permit issued by the Florida Department of Transportation. The gross weight of the vehicle and its cargo was about 150,000 lbs. Investigation indicated that the distance between the semitrailer's kingpin and the first semitrailer axle was 31 feet, 9 inches, and in this configuration the underside of the semitrailer's cargo bed cleared a level roadway by about 9 1/2 inches. The crossing had an average 3-percent upgrade for 100 feet to the track centerline east of the track, and had an average 4-percent downgrade for 100 feet from the track centerline west of the track.

The 31-year-old truckdriver reported that he had taken delivery of the lowbed semitrailer the day before the accident. The semitrailer had been lodged over the crossing for about 15 minutes, during which time the driver and a helper had attempted to use the hydraulic lift on the semitrailer to get it off the crossing. They did not attempt to contact the police or the railroad before the collision. When they heard the train approaching, the helper ran down the tracks and attempted to stop the train while the driver entered the cab and made a last attempt to move the unit. He jumped from the cab immediately before the collision and was not injured.

CASE NO. 3

Safety Board Investigation Number:	FTW-85-F-X025
Accident Location:	Deadwood Road, Donner (Schriever), Louisiana
Date and Time:	September 4, 1985, 4:06 p.m.
Motor Vehicle Type:	Tractor/lowbed semitrailer
Motor Carrier:	Sampey Brothers, Ltd., Morgan City, Louisiana
Train Involved:	Amtrak, Train No. 1
Railroad Involved:	Southern Pacific Transportation Company
U.S. DOT/AAR Crossing Number:	758075V
Train-Activated Warning Devices:	None (crossbucks and stop sign only)
Fatalities:	0
Injuries:	0
Estimated Property Damage:	$40,000

Summary:

Amtrak train No. 1 was traveling southbound about 70 mph when the engineer and the fireman on the lead unit noticed a lowbed semitrailer on the Deadwood Road grade crossing. The train's engineer initiated an emergency application of the brakes, reducing the speed of the train to about 40 mph when it struck the semitrailer. The semitrailer was propelled about 150 feet and struck a parked, unoccupied pickup truck. The train did not derail, and only the front end of the lead unit was damaged. The crew members and 93 passengers onboard were not injured.

The 42-foot long semitrailer, transporting a bulldozer, had hung up on the hump crossing as the vehicle was traveling east on Deadwood Road about 5 minutes before the train arrived. The truck tractor had begun descending a 5.8-percent downgrade while the lowbed semitrailer was still on a 13.5-percent upgrade, and the semitrailer lodged on the crossing. After becoming lodged, the driver had detached the tractor, unloaded the bulldozer, and was attempting to use the bulldozer to free the semitrailer when the collision occurred. The nearest phone was four miles away, and the driver made no attempt to contact the police or the railroad before the collision.

The distance between the rear axle on the tractor and the first axle on the semitrailer was 28 feet, and the vehicle had a ground clearance of 8 inches between these axles. According to a Louisiana State statute, the ground clearance should have been 14 inches for that configuration.

CASE NO. 4

Safety Board Investigation Number: CHI-87-H-TR04
Accident Location: Clay Street, Gary, Indiana
Date and Time: October 30, 1986, 6:40 p.m.
Motor Vehicle Type: Tractor/lowbed semitrailer
Motor Carrier: Diamond Bell Express, Inc.
Train Involved: Commuter Rail Passenger Train No. 119
Railroad Involved: Chicago, Southshore, and South Bend Railroad

U.S. DOT/AAR Crossing Number: 870879M
Train-Activated Warning Devices: Red flashing lights, gates

Fatalities: 0
Injuries: 32
Estimated Property Damage: $110,000

Summary:

An eastbound Chicago, Southshore, and South Bend Railroad electric passenger train was operating at an engineer-reported 45 mph approaching the Clay Street grade crossing in Gary, Indiana, when the engineer saw a truck blocking the tracks. He applied the brakes but was unable to stop in time to avoid the collision. The collision separated the tractor from the semitrailer and its cargo, and the semitrailer came to rest 232 feet east of the crossing. At impact, the 38,190-pound steel coil the truck was transporting penetrated the head end of the first car in the train consist and rolled down the center aisle of the car, coming to rest about 1/2 way through the occupied car.

The semitrailer was designed with a hydraulic cargo bed which, after being positioned under a cradled steel coil, was raised, lifting both the coil and the cradle off the ground about 8 inches for transport. The distance between the semitrailer's kingpin and the first semitrailer axle was about 31 feet, 9 inches.

The 52-year-old truckdriver had 2 1/2 years experience driving this type vehicle. He reported that the drive shaft snapped when he tried to drag the semitrailer over the hump crossing and that he had been stopped on the crossing 10 to 15 minutes when the collision occurred. While lodged on the crossing, he was clearing traffic so that another Diamond Bell unit he knew was traveling behind him could tow him off the crossing. When the warning devices activated, he tried to use a flashlight to signal the approaching train to stop, but was unable to prevent the collision.

The motor carrier was using this humped crossing in place of another level crossing in order to avoid confrontations in crossing a Steelworker's Union picket line. The carrier had experienced problems in clearing the accident crossing in the recent past, and had equipped its lowbed vehicles with two-way radios to reach the carrier's dispatcher in case a vehicle fouled this crossing so that the dispatcher could call the railroad. The radio was found to be inoperative after the accident, and the driver made no attempt to contact the police or the railroad by telephone before the collision.

CASE NO. 5

Safety Board Investigation Number:	ATL-87-H-TR02
Accident Location:	Fellwood Road, College Park, Georgia
Date and Time:	November 12, 1986, 7:22 a.m.
Motor Vehicle Type:	Tractor/lowbed auto transporter
Motor Carrier:	Pensacola Auto Auction, Pensacola, Florida
Train Involved:	CSXT Freight Train No. M-615-12
Railroad Involved:	CSX Transportation, Inc.
U.S. DOT/AAR Crossing Number:	N/A
Train-Activated Warning Devices:	Flashing lights, gates, bells
Fatalities:	0
Injuries:	0
Estimated Property Damage:	$90,000

Summary:

CSXT train No. M-615-12 was traveling southbound at an engineer-reported speed of 48-50 mph. When the lead unit was about 1,500 feet north of the Fellwood Road grade crossing, the engineer noticed a truck on the crossing and began sounding the horn. When the lead unit was about 900 feet from the crossing, the engineer determined the truck was lodged on the humped crossing. He stopped sounding the horn, applied the brakes in emergency, and he and the brakeman then lay on the floor until the crash occurred. The train did not derail and stopped with the first freight car across Fellwood Road.

The 26-year-old truckdriver had been driving the accident vehicle for about 10 months. While en route to make a delivery, he had turned onto westbound Fellwood Road and failed to heed a sign prohibiting trucks over 30 feet in length on that roadway. After the center of the semitrailer became lodged on the humped grade crossing, he spent 20 minutes stopping passing motorists and using his CB radio in an attempt to get a tow truck to pull him off the crossing. He made no attempt to contact the police or the railroad by telephone before the collision.

After receiving notification on his CB that a freight train was traveling toward the crossing, he saw the headlight of the approaching train. He then ran north along the track and attempted to flag the train down, but the train passed him. He then saw the crossing warning devices activate and witnessed the collision.

The distance between the semitrailer's kingpin and the first semitrailer axle was about 31 feet. There was 10 inches clearance between a level roadway and the underside of the semitrailer's cargo bed.

CASE NO. 6

Safety Board Investigation Number:	LAX-87-F-XO06 / SEA-87-H-TR03
Accident Location:	Walnut Street, Winlock, Washington
Date and Time:	December 22, 1986, 1:30 p.m.
Motor Vehicle Type:	Tractor/lowbed semitrailer
Motor Carrier:	M&M Transport Company
	Chehalis, Washington
Train Involved:	Amtrak Train No.11
Railroad Involved:	Burlington Northern Railroad Company
U.S. DOT/AAR Crossing Number:	(BN milepost 71.43)
Train-Activated Warning Devices:	Crossing gates, flashing red lights, bells
Fatalities:	0
Injuries:	3
Estimated Property Damage:	$252,000

Summary:

Amtrak train No. 11 was traveling southbound when the engineer in the lead unit noticed an eastbound tractor-semitrailer stopped over the double-track main line at the Walnut Street grade crossing. He made an emergency brake application and sounded the horn before striking the left side of the tractor at the fifth wheel. The lead locomotive event recorder indicated that the speed at impact was 51 mph.

The impact derailed the two locomotives and four of the thirteen coaches. The diesel tank on the second locomotive unit was punctured. The semitrailer was torn in two, spilling its cargo of wood chips. The tractor and the front portion of the semitrailer were pushed 168 feet down the track and came to rest upright, blocking the northbound main track. The rear portion of the semitrailer knocked over the crossing signal southwest of the crossing and came to rest 50 feet south of the point of impact. Two train passengers and one traincrew member sustained minor injuries.

The 36-year-old truckdriver had 7 months' experience driving the unit. The driver stated he stopped before the crossing, shifted into second gear, and increased engine speed to 1,800 rpm to get over the humped tracks. He also stated that after becoming lodged on the crossing, he tried unsuccessfully to move the vehicle for about 2 1/2 minutes until he saw the train approaching. He did not attempt to contact the police or the railroad before the collision.

Walnut Street (State Route 603) on its western approach to the grade crossing had a 14-percent ascending grade beginning 64 feet west of the most western rail which continued to 5 feet west of the rail where the grade transitioned to a 5-percent ascending grade. The semitrailer had a ground clearance of 12 inches.

CASE NO. 7

Safety Board Investigation Numbers:	DEN-87-F-X005/SEA-87-H-TR04
Accident Location:	East Territorial Road, near Canby, Oregon
Date and Time:	January 15, 1987, 1:00 p.m.
Motor Vehicle Type:	Tractor/lowbed semitrailer
Motor Carrier:	Grey's International of Oregon, Inc.
Train Involved:	Amtrak Train No.14
Railroad Involved:	Southern Pacific Railroad Company
U.S. DOT/AAR Crossing Number:	(SP Milepost 748.70)
Train-Activated Warning Devices:	Crossing gates, flashing red lights, bells
Fatalities:	0
Injuries:	1
Estimated Property Damage:	$49,022

Summary:

Amtrak train No. 14 was traveling northbound at 65-70 mph when the engineer noticed an object ahead over the tracks at the East Territorial Road grade crossing. He made an initial speed reduction, and then went to emergency braking when he saw a man waving his arms and running down the tracks toward the train. The engineer estimated that the train's speed had been reduced to about 35 mph when the collision occurred.

The collision caused the rear wheels of the second locomotive unit to derail, and the train pushed the tractor and semitrailer more that 400 feet down the track. The semitrailer's load of crane parts was knocked off the semitrailer at impact and dragged along with the vehicle. The front of the lead locomotive came to rest approximately 595 feet north of the crossing. One of the 207 passengers sustained a minor injury. The truckdriver was not injured.

The 52-year-old truckdriver had 20 years' experience driving this type vehicle. After the vehicle had lodged on the track for about 2 minutes, the crossing warning devices activated, and the driver exited the vehicle and tried to flag the approaching train. The tractor was equipped with a two-way radio which he could have used to reach the motor carrier's office, but the driver did not use it before the collision.

The eastbound approach to the crossing at East Territorial Road had a 5.8-percent ascending grade for 40 feet, transitioning to a 12.6-percent ascending grade the final 3 feet to the tracks. Westbound, the roadway has a 3.2-percent descending grade for 42 feet. The semitrailer had a ground clearance of 7 3/4 inches.

CASE NO. 8

Safety Board Investigation Number:	ATL-87-H-TR03
Accident Location:	State Road 125, Halifax, North Carolina
Date and Time:	November 12, 1987, 1:50 p.m.
Motor Vehicle Type:	Tractor/lowbed semitrailer
Motor Carrier:	Daniels Transfer Company, Inc. Franklin, Pennsylvania
Train Involved:	CSXT Freight Train R460
Railroad Involved:	Seaboard System Railroad (Operated by CSX Transportation, Inc.)
U.S. DOT/AAR Crossing Number:	629659J
Train-Activated Warning Devices:	Flashing lights, gates
Fatalities:	0
Injuries:	0
Estimated Property Damage:	$266,130

Summary:

CSXT freight train R460 was traveling northbound on the Seaboard System Railroad when the engineer observed an eastbound lowbed semitrailer over the North Carolina S.R. 125 and a person waving his arms and running toward the train. The engineer initiated an emergency brake application, but the train struck the right side of the hung-up semitrailer. The train had no speed recording equipment, but the engineer estimated that the speed of the train was about 50 mph at the time of the collision.

The impact caused the lead engine of the train to derail several yards north of the crossing, and 8 of the 134 freight cars also derailed. The track sustained extensive damage. The semitrailer and its cargo, a Caterpillar excavator, were thrown to the northeast quadrant of the crossing. The semitrailer and the excavator were extensively damaged, and the excavator separated from the semitrailer's cargo deck.

The semitrailer had been lodged over the crossing for 5 to 10 minutes before the collision. During that time, the driver attempted to drive the unit from the crossing, but was unsuccessful. Another truck had stopped behind the lodged semitrailer, and the two truckdrivers were discussing the possibility of pulling it off the crossing when they noticed the approaching train. The truckdriver ran south and attempted to flag the train, but was unsuccessful. He did not attempt to contact the police or the railroad before the collision.

The truckdriver had 29 years' over-the-road truckdriving experience, including considerable experience operating lowbed semitrailers.

CASE NO. 9

Safety Board Investigation Number:	ATL-88-F-FX007
Accident Location:	Lenna Avenue, Seffner, Florida
Date and Time:	November 25, 1987, 10:25 a.m.
Motor Vehicle Type:	Tractor/lowbed semitrailer
Motor Carrier:	U. S. Boring and Tunneling, Bartow, Florida
Train Involved:	Amtrak, Train No. 81 (Silver Star)
Railroad Involved:	CSX Transportation, Inc.
U.S. DOT/AAR Crossing Number:	624349X
Train-Activated Warning Devices:	Flashing lights, gates, bells
Fatalities:	0
Injuries:	17
Estimated Property Damage:	$336,349

Summary:

Amtrak train No. 81 was traveling westbound at a reported speed of 70 mph when it rounded a curve and the engineer and fireman observed a northbound tractor-lowbed semitrailer transporting a backhoe stopped over the Lenna Avenue grade crossing. The engineer made a service brake application, then made an emergency brake application when he determined that the truck was not moving off the crossing. The engineer and the fireman evacuated the cab into the engine room.

The engineer estimated the train was traveling about 40 to 50 mph when it struck the semitrailer. The locomotive derailed and overturned onto its right side, and a baggage and sleeping car derailed. The tractor was damaged and the semitrailer and backhoe were destroyed.

The 28-year-old truckdriver had 7 1/2 years' experience in operating commercial vehicles, including tractor-lowbed semitrailer combinations. At the time of the accident he was traveling over the crossing at the direction of his foreman, who was on the ground north of the crossing directing the truck's movements.

The truckdriver stated that as he drove over the crossing he felt a rocking motion and the tractor's engine stalled. He restarted the engine, heard the crossing bells activate, and attempted to back off the crossing, stalling the engine again. He restarted the engine again, locked the differential, and noted that the tractor's drive wheels were spinning. He then exited the cab immediately before the collision.

Postaccident tests indicated the vertical road clearance of a similar unloaded semitrailer was 9 inches. This dimension decreased to 5.25 inches at maximum rated load of 35 tons.

CASE NO. 10

Safety Board Investigation Number:	WRH-91-F-H001
Accident Location:	Leucadia Boulevard, Encinitas, California
Date and Time:	October 3, 1990, 2:44 p.m.
Motor Vehicle Type:	Tractor/auto transporter semitrailer
Motor Carrier:	Time Auto Transport, Troy, Michigan
Train Involved:	Amtrak Train No. 576
Railroad Involved:	Atchison, Topeka, and Santa Fe Railway Company (ATSF)
U.S. DOT/AAR Crossing Number:	026827V
Train-Activated Warning Devices:	Crossing gates, flashing red lights
Fatalities:	0
Injuries:	13
Estimated Property Damage:	$285,000

Summary:

Amtrak train No. 576 was traveling southbound at 90 mph on the ATSF single-track main line en route to San Diego from Los Angeles when the engineer saw something across the track at the Leucadia Boulevard grade crossing. Seconds later, he realized that it was a tractor-auto transporter semitrailer and that it was not moving. The engineer sounded the horn, and about 1,000 feet before the crossing he began an emergency brake application. He then exited the cab of the control car (the locomotive was at the rear of the consist, in the push mode). The train struck the semitrailer at about 65 mph.

The collision caused the cab control car to derail, but it remained upright. The front section of the cab control car was damaged substantially, and 13 of the 71 persons aboard the train were injured. The truck tractor was not damaged, but the auto transporter semitrailer was severed. The front portion of the semitrailer rotated about 90 degrees and came to rest upright, and the remainder of the unit came to rest south of the crossing. Five of the eight vehicles on the semitrailer were torn from it, and two of those were destroyed. Three vehicles remained on the semitrailer and were not damaged.

The combination unit had been traveling westbound on Leucadia Boulevard when the bottom of the semitrailer had become lodged at the crossing. The driver attempted to dislodge the vehicle, but his efforts failed. He and his co-driver exited the vehicle, and they walked to a convenience store about 200 feet away to call for help. While he was on the phone, the driver heard the train's whistle. He left the store and saw the train strike the semitrailer. He estimated the semitrailer had been lodged over the track for 10 to 13 minutes before the collision.

The 27-year-old driver of the auto carrier failed to heed a sign indicating that no trucks were allowed which was posted for westbound Leucadia Boulevard vehicles 3/8 mile before the crossing. He stated he did not see the sign. Alternate approved truck routes existed at crossings north and south of Leucadia Boulevard. Westbound Leucadia Boulevard at the crossing had a 2-percent ascending grade that begins 13 feet 7 inches east of the track centerline. The tracks were level. Beginning 4 feet 7 inches west of the track centerline, the roadway descended at a 9-percent grade for 4 feet 6 inches, then descended at a 7-percent grade for 32 feet. The semitrailer manufacturer advised that the as-built clearance of the cargo deck on a level roadway was about 7 1/2 inches.

The San Diego County Sheriff's Department first received notice of the vehicle lodged on the track via a 911 call at 2:41 p.m. The collision occurred 3 minutes later while the sheriff's office was looking up a toll-free emergency number previously supplied to the office by the ATSF and listed in its computerized records. After the accident had occurred, the sheriff's office placed two calls, at 2:49 and 2:50 p.m. respectively, to the ASTF toll-free number; however, the line was busy both times because the toll-free number was also being used for general railroad business, and it did not have the roll-over capability to handle additional incoming calls. When the sheriff's office did establish contact with ATSF, at 2:51 p.m., the ASTF's Regional Operations Center at San Bernardino, California, had already been notified of the accident via radio by the conductor on the train.

After this accident, ASTF changed its telephone system so that incoming calls to the emergency number would roll over when the line was busy to a red phone located between two supervisors on duty. No outgoing calls could be made on this red phone. Also after the accident, the City of Encinitas posted signs reading "Railroad Emergencies Call 911" east and west of the Leucadia Boulevard crossing.

CASE NO. 11

Safety Board Investigation Number:	NYC-92-F-RO21
Accident Location:	Orchard Road, East Patchoque, New York
Date and Time:	May 11, 1992, 6:35 a.m.
Motor Vehicle Type:	Tractor/lowbed semitrailer
Motor Carrier:	Pilato Trucking, Massapequa, New York
Train Involved:	Long Island Railroad Passenger Train No.11
Railroad Involved:	Long Island Railroad, Montauk Branch
U.S. DOT/AAR Crossing Number:	3380596 (?)
Train-Activated Warning Devices:	Gates, bells, flashing red lights
Fatalities:	0
Injuries:	28
Estimated Property Damage:	$173,837

Summary:

Long Island Railroad passenger train No. 11 was traveling at 55 to 60 mph westbound on the Montauk Branch en route to Babylon, New York, when the engineer observed a tractor semitrailer combination unit loaded with four concrete sewer vaults lodged on the track at the Orchard Road grade crossing. He sounded the horn several times. When the lead unit was about 600 feet away from the crossing, the engineer noted that the truck was not moving, and he made an emergency brake application. At about the same time, he saw a man running toward the train waving his arms. The train was unable to stop before it struck the semitrailer at an estimated speed of 45 mph.

The lead locomotive derailed as a result of the impact, coming to rest north of the tracks about 300 feet from the crossing. The locomotive sustained extensive damage, as did the signal and crossing protection devices. The semitrailer was shoved to the south of the track, and two of the four concrete units on the semitrailer were shattered. The truck tractor came to rest north of the crossing 25 feet west of the point of impact. Minor injuries were sustained by 24 passengers and the train's crew of 4.

The truckdriver stated he came to a full stop at the track, and then proceeded to cross. When the combination unit was about halfway across the track, the semitrailer became lodged on one of the rails. The driver had spent about 4 minutes attempting to move the vehicle when he noticed the crossing protection being activated by the approaching train. He abandoned the vehicle and ran towards the train, trying to flag it down. He did not attempt to call the police or the railroad before the collision.

The southbound approach to the crossing had a 4-percent upgrade, while the north side of the track has a 0.3-percent downgrade. The semitrailer had a ground clearance of 7 inches.

CASE NO. 12

Safety Board Investigation Number:	SRH-92-F-HO21
Accident Location:	Woodland Drive, near Orange Park, Florida
Date and Time:	June 30, 1992, 12:15 p.m.
Motor Vehicle Type:	Tractor/household goods van semitrailer
Motor Carrier:	Suddath Van Lines, Jacksonville, Florida
Train Involved:	CSXT Freight Train No. N00129
Railroad Involved:	CSX Transportation, Inc.
DOT/AAR Crossing Number:	620906T
Train-Activated Warning Devices:	Flashing lights, gates
Fatalities:	0
Injuries:	0
Estimated Property Damage:	$169,000

Summary:

CSXT freight train No. N00129 was proceeding southbound around a 3-degree right curve when the engineer observed a moving van blocking the track at the Woodland Drive grade crossing. Sight distance to the crossing from where the engineer could have first observed the van was about 1,000 feet, and the engineer reported he rounded the curve at about 40 mph. The engineer reported he made an emergency brake application. The train struck the midsection of the van semitrailer, tearing it in two. The front of the semitrailer remained coupled to the tractor, and the rear section came to rest south of the crossing and west of the track. The semitrailer's cargo of used household goods was strewn along the track south of the crossing and were mostly destroyed. The train remained in line and on the track, and the lead unit stopped 1,080 feet south of the crossing. The three occupants of the tractor semitrailer combination unit and the three crewmembers onboard the train were not injured.

The moving van had become lodged on the humped crossing at 11:45 a.m., some 30 minutes before the collision. The tractor-semitrailer had an overall length of 59 feet, a distance of 32 feet 3 inches between common suspension points, and a ground clearance of approximately 14 inches. The tractor began descending a 7.3-percent downgrade while the semitrailer was still on a 5.3-percent upgrade., causing the semitrailer to lodge over the tracks.

After the semitrailer hung up, the three occupants, a driver and two passengers, exited the vehicle and made a brief inspection before beginning efforts to contact the police to obtain assistance in moving the lodged vehicle from the track.

The Clay County Sheriff's Office received notification of the lodged vehicle at 11:50 a.m., and dispatched a deputy who arrived on-scene at 11:59 a.m. At 12:00 p.m., the sheriff's office notified CSXT central dispatch in Jacksonville, Florida, of the vehicle lodged at the Woodland Drive crossing.

Meanwhile, the proprietor of a local business, based upon erroneous information received from a customer, called the Orange Park Police Department (OPPD) and advised there was a truck lodged on the tracks at Kingsley Avenue, 2.5 miles north of Woodland Drive, within the City of Orange Park. At 12:02 p.m. the OPPD dispatcher telephoned this information to CSXT in Jacksonville. The CSXT dispatcher asked the police dispatcher if the call was about the truck lodged on a crossing. The police dispatcher responded affirmatively, and the CSXT dispatcher advised "We already know about it."

An OPPD officer traveled to the Kingsley Avenue crossing. Finding it clear, he checked and determined that the other four grade crossings in the City of Orange Park were also clear. At 12:08 p.m. the OPPD telephoned CSXT Jacksonville and advised there was no truck hung up at the "Kingsley Avenue crossing or any other grade crossing in Orange Park."

After receipt of this telephone call, CSXT issued an "all clear" signal to train N00129. The collision occurred about 7 minutes later.

CASE NO. 13

Safety Board Investigation Number:	DCA-93-M-HO02
Accident Location:	Kissimmee Utility Authority (KUA) Power Road, Intercession City, Florida
Date and Time:	November 30, 1993, 12:40 p.m.
Motor Vehicle Type:	Tractor/lowbed modular unit semitrailer
Motor Carrier:	Rountree Transport and Rigging, Inc.,
Train Involved:	Amtrak Train No. 88, (Silver Meteor)
Railroad Involved:	CSX Transportation, Inc.
U.S. DOT/AAR Crossing Number:	643879N
Train-Activated Warning Devices:	Flashing lights, gates, bells
Fatalities:	0
Injuries:	59
Estimated Property Damage:	$14,000,000

Summary:

Amtrak train No. 88 was traveling eastbound at an engineer-reported speed of 79 mph rounding a 1-degree curve to the right when the engineer observed a large object ahead. As the train approached the KUA Power Road grade crossing and the object came into clear view, the engineer saw that the object was over the tracks and he made an emergency brake application. The engineer and the assistant engineer evacuated the locomotive's control compartment through the auxiliary engine compartment door.

The object over the tracks ahead was a lowbed semitrailer loaded with a turbine generator that was being transported to an electric generating plant under construction. The turbine itself was 57 feet long and 17 feet high, and its 13-axle transport vehicle combination was 184 feet long. The gross weight of the transport vehicle and its cargo was 291,000 pounds. The vehicle had been stopped while over the tracks and its three-person crew was raising the cargo deck to clear the hump in the road about 34 feet north of the tracks.

The locomotive collided with the center of the turbine and the vehicle's cargo deck at a speed calculated to be about 54 mph. The locomotive and the first four cars of the eight-car consist derailed, and the train continued eastward about 344 feet, carrying parts of the transport vehicle and the turbine with it. The locomotive overturned, came to rest on its left side, and sustained extensive damage. Three railroad cars were extensively damaged, and the turbine, transport vehicle, and track and signals east of the crossing were destroyed. The engineer, assistant engineer, truckdriver, and 56 of the train's passengers and on-board service crewmembers were injured.

The north rail on the railroad was superelevated 3 inches above the south rail, and the tracks were above the surrounding terrain. To cross the tracks at grade, the KUA Power Road was constructed in the summer of 1993 with an average 3.8-percent ascending grade beginning about 87 feet south of the south rail. North of the tracks, the roadway continued to ascend for about 34 feet to the high point of the roadway. North of the high point the roadway had an average 4.4-percent descending grade back to the level of the surrounding terrain.

The hump in the roadway was located more than 30 feet north of the tracks to prevent most lowbed vehicles from becoming lodged on the hump while part of the vehicle was still over the tracks. This method of construction is in substantial compliance with guidelines established by the American Railway Engineering Association (AREA) and the American Association of State Highway and Transportation Officials (AASHTO) which were adopted as construction standards for public roads by the Federal Highway Administration effective June 1, 1993.

Because of the unusual configuration of the modular transport vehicle, with a span of 83 1/4 feet between axles 7 and 8 and with a normal ground clearance of about 8 inches over that distance, the cargo deck between axles 7 and 8 could not clear the hump north of the tracks, and the vehicle had to be stopped with the cargo deck and the turbine over the tracks while the cargo deck was raised to clear the hump.

While efforts were being made to raise the cargo deck, the supervisor in charge of the modular transporter made several attempts to telephone the railroad using his cellular phone. He reported that about 7 minutes before the collision he attempted to contact a CSXT trainmaster, but the phone was not answered. He then attempted twice to reach the railroad at another number and received only a pre-recorded message. Neither number was suitable for calling the railroad to report an emergency, and he was still attempting to telephone the railroad when he heard the whistle of the approaching train.

CASE NO. 14

Safety Board Investigation Number:	SRH-95-MH-026
Accident Location:	Boogaloo Road, near Sycamore, South Carolina
Date and Time:	May 2, 1995, 2:35 a.m.
Motor Vehicle Type:	Tractor/lowbed semitrailer
Motor Carrier:	O&J Gordon Trucking, Estill, South Carolina
Train Involved:	Amtrak Train No. 81 (Silver Star)
Railroad Involved:	CSX Transportation, Inc.
U.S. DOT/AAR Crossing Number:	634810U
Train-Activated Warning Devices:	None (crossbucks only)
Fatalities:	0
Injuries:	33
Estimated Property Damage:	$1,000,000

Summary

Amtrak train No. 81 was traveling southbound at an engineer-reported speed of 79 mph when the engineer, who was riding on the left side of the lead locomotive, reported he first saw a person on or near the west track waving his arms, and then immediately thereafter saw a semitrailer over the tracks. He made an immediate emergency brake application and then he fell to the floor.

The lead locomotive struck the right front of the semitrailer, separating the semitrailer from the tractor. The assistant engineer, who was operating the train at the time of the accident, was thrown to the floor of the control cab at impact. The impact rotated the semitrailer counterclockwise, and the rear of the semitrailer collided with the second truck on the lead locomotive. The 2 locomotive units and first 14 cars of the 18-car consist then derailed. The semitrailer came to rest southwest of the crossing with the front facing north. The tractor and semitrailer were substantially damaged.

The truckdriver reported that, while he had towed the accident semitrailer before this trip, he had never driven with it over this crossing. He had previously traveled over the accident crossing towing another lowbed semitrailer with no problems, but the accident semitrailer had less road clearance than the lowbed he usually towed. After the semitrailer lodged on the crossing, the driver tried to pull forward and backward, and tried to uncouple the semitrailer, but was unsuccessful in these efforts. He reported he had been lodged on the crossing for about 35 minutes when he saw the headlight of the approaching train.

The westbound approach to the humped crossing has an average 9.9-percent ascending grade over the last 30 feet before reaching the east rail, and after crossing the tracks the westbound roadway has an average descending grade of 3.5-percent over the first 30 feet of roadway west of the west rail.

CASE NO. 15

Safety Board Investigation Number:	SRH-95-F-HO27
Accident Location:	Graysville Road, Graysville, Georgia
Date and Time:	May 10, 1995, 8:58 p.m.
Motor Vehicle Type:	Tractor/lowbed semitrailer
Motor Carrier:	JWT, Inc, Chattanooga, Tennessee
Train Involved:	CSXT Freight Train No. R58310
Railroad Involved:	CSX Transportation, Inc.
U.S. DOT/AAR Crossing Number:	340584H
Train-Activated Warning Devices: Flashing lights, gates, bells	

Fatalities:	0
Injuries:	1
Estimated Property Damage:	$1,000,000

Summary:

CSXT Freight train No. R58310, consisting of four locomotives and 110 cars, was traveling southbound about 45 mph en route from Chattanooga, Tennessee, to Atlanta, Georgia. The conductor, seated on the east side of the control cab, stated that as the train came out of a right-hand curve about 750 feet from the crossing, both he and the engineer saw a semitrailer across the tracks. At that point, the engineer made an emergency brake application and yelled for the conductor to hit the floor. After impact, the conductor checked to see if the engineer was hurt and then attempted to contact the dispatcher via radio, but could not do so because of static on the radio. Both he and the engineer were covered with fuel from the ruptured fuel tanks of the locomotive. The conductor sustained minor injuries.

The truckdriver stated he was stuck on the crossing 5 to 10 minutes before the collision. As soon as he got stuck, his passenger got out of the truck to see where they were hung up. Within 1 minute of the time the truck became stuck on the crossing, a Catoosa County sheriff's deputy arrived on the scene. advised that a train was coming, and urged the driver to expedite efforts to get the truck off the crossing. The deputy then parked his cruiser behind the truck and alerted motorists to stay clear of the area. As the deputy was talking on the radio to his dispatcher, the dispatcher could hear the train horn in the background. A passerby also dialed 911 on his cellular telephone, reaching the Chattanooga Police Department, who also relayed information about the lodged truck to the Catoosa County dispatcher.

Although the sheriff's dispatcher reached the railroad before the collision, there was insufficient time to stop the train. The 60,000 lb. backhoe the truck was transporting was destroyed.

Eastbound Graysville Road passes over two tracks, the main line track and a passing track. The roadway is a 3-percent ascending grade to the main line track at the high point of the crossing, then the roadway begins an average 8-percent descending grade for 30 feet. The passing track is about 18 inches lower than the main line track.

CASE NO. 16

Safety Board Investigation Number:	SRH-96-MH-001
Accident Location:	Plains Road, Milford, Connecticut
Date and Time:	October 3, 1995, 7:13 a.m.
Motor Vehicle Type:	Tractor/lowbed semitrailer
Motor Carrier:	J. D. C. Trucking, Inc., Newington, Connecticut
Train Involved:	Metro North Commuter Train No. 1933
Railroad Involved:	Metro North Railroad
U.S. DOT/AAR Crossing Number:	503877P
Train-Activated Warning Devices:	Red flashing lights, gates, bells
Fatalities:	0
Injuries:	24
Estimated Property Damage:	$500,000

Summary:

A Metro North Railroad Commuter Train consisting of a control car, a passenger car, and a locomotive operating in the push mode was traveling southbound on the Metro North Waterbury Branch at an engineer-reported speed of 59 mph. As the train traveled around a left-hand curve, the Plains Road grade crossing came into sight about 1,800 feet ahead and the engineer in the control car noticed an eastbound tractor-semitrailer over the crossing.

The engineer initiated a braking action, and seconds later when he determined that the truck wasn't moving, initiated an emergency brake application. He then exited the control cab, warned the passengers in the lead car of the impending collision, and braced himself.

The lead car in the consist struck the lowbed semitrailer and the excavator it was transporting. The collision separated the tractor from the semitrailer and its cargo, an excavator. The first truck of the lead car overrode the semitrailer, pushing the excavator off the semitrailer and east of the tracks. The lead car then carried the semitrailer with it as it traveled south of the crossing where it came to rest with its lead truck derailed.

The gross weight of the highway vehicle and its cargo was 110,000 pounds. The excavator was being transported from Newington, Connecticut, to a job site in Milford, Connecticut. Although the motor carrier had obtained a special permit from Connecticut, the truck was traveling on an unauthorized route when it became lodged on the hump crossing.

The eastbound approach to the crossing had an average 9.1-percent ascending grade beginning 28 feet from the west rail, and the eastbound departure had an average 3.7-percent descending grade from the east rail.

The 30-year-old truckdriver reported that after becoming lodged on the crossing he attempted to raise the semitrailer frame by operating the hydraulic ram on the gooseneck, but was unsuccessful in this attempt in the 3 to 4 minutes between his becoming lodged on the crossing and the approach of the train. Neither the driver nor any other passersby or witnesses attempted to contact the police or the railroad during this time, although the crossing was posted with signs advising the public as follows:

TO REPORT MALFUNCTION
OF SIGNALS
CALL 911
CROSSING
I.D.#503877P
PLAINS RD

APPENDIX F

U.S. Department of Transportation Related Items
on Emergency Notification Systems

Federal Railroad Administration (FRA): In October 1994, the U.S. Congress passed the High-Speed Rail Development Act of 1994 (the Swift Rail Development Act). Title III, Section 301 of the Swift Rail Development Act included a provision for a pilot automated emergency notification system.[1] Section 301 provides that the Secretary of Transportation shall conduct a pilot program to demonstrate an emergency notification system utilizing a toll free telephone number that the public can use to convey to railroad carriers, either directly or through public safety personnel, information about malfunctions or other safety problems at railroad-highway grade crossings.

Congress set as a minimum that the program should:
include railroad-highway grade crossings in at least two states;
include provisions for public education and awareness of program; and
require information to be posted at the railroad-highway grade crossing describing the emergency notification system and instructions on how to use the system.

No appropriations were authorized to pay for this demonstration.

U.S. Department of Transportation (DOT): In 1994, the DOT released an action plan that addresses improving highway/rail crossing safety. One area of this plan called for improved research and data. Under this broad area, the DOT included a proposal for a 1-800 Computer Answering System stating "...an automated telephone answering and message forwarding system will be developed for handling calls concerning malfunctions or problems at highway/rail grade crossings."

The plan goes further in proposing that the FRA will hold an informal safety inquiry to consider requiring the display of the U.S. DOT/AAR Inventory number and a toll free phone number at all crossings to facilitate emergency notification.[2]

Currently, the FRA project manager is attempting to secure funding and identify two States willing to undertake the demonstration program stipulated in the Swift Rail Development Act and the DOT Action Plan. The estimated start-up costs for this fully automated 1-800 Automated Crossing Trouble Report System are estimated at $750,000. To date, funds have not been secured, and only one State, Minnesota, has indicated a willingness to install a statewide system if funding becomes available.

---

[1]Public Law 103-440 enacted November 2, 1994, 108 STAT.4626, 103rd Congress.
[2]See *Conceptual Design and Implementation Plan for an Automated 1-800 Crossing Trouble Report System*, prepared by AMB Associates, Inc., under contract DTFR53-92-C-00047, Modification #13, dated May 19, 1995.

Actual implementation of the FRA system will entail entering the DOT/AAR inventory and integrating contact data consisting of railroad and public safety telephone numbers. Currently, this system's proposal includes an interactive voice response feature that will handle automated telephone answering functions and unattended interactions with callers, capture and process information provided by callers, and generate and fax "trouble reports" to railroads and/or public safety officials. It also is proposed that a supplemental system allowing callers to interact with a live attendant be made available, particularly for an immediate emergency.

A major component of this system will be signs posted at grade crossings. The FRA plans to have signs posted at all public grade crossings (active and passive) and at private grade crossings with active warning devices. These signs will prominently display a 1-800 toll-free telephone number that individuals can use to call and report signal malfunctions or other crossing problems. The grade crossings will be identified by the DOT/AAR inventory number.

The FRA anticipates that this pilot project will lead to a fully operational national system with States being gradually included into the system at their option. This recognizes that some States, such as Texas, Delaware, and Connecticut, may have their own systems and may not wish to join the national network.

In a separate action, the FRA has requested that the FHWA amend Part VIII of the *Manual of Uniform Control Devices* standards for the design and placement of a DOT/AAR inventory plate. FRA's proposal specifies the sign size, the material to be used, and the location of the plate at the crossing.[3]

An upcoming Safety Board study on passive grade crossings will address these issues from a global perspective. In 1996, the Board will conduct a safety study on passive grade crossings. Staff will investigate about 60 accidents at grade crossings that are not equipped with train-activated warning devices. The study will document the current state of safety at passive grade crossings and explore ways in which collisions between highway vehicles and trains can be prevented at these crossings. The study will document ways to reduce the number of accidents through regulatory initiatives, educational programs, new technology, and low-cost physical improvements to the crossing.

---

[3]See DOT, FHWA, 23 CFR Part 655, [FHWA Docket No. 95-8], National Standards for Traffic Control Devices; Revision of the Manual on Traffic Control Devices, Notice of Proposed Amendments, 60 FR 31035-31036 dated June 12, 1995.